THE COV]

The beautiful cover design for this book, by Mr. Gurney Benham, of Colchester, deserves some slight description. It contains the arms of the famous William of Wykeham, Bishop of Winchester, and those of New College, Oxford, which adopted the Bishop's arms and motto, impaling his armorial bearings with those of the see of Winchester. The close connection of William of Wykeham and of New College with the fortunes of Hornchurch is mentioned on page 61. The Other arms shown in this cover design include those traditionally assigned to Edward the Confessor (see p. 56) and to the Kings of the East Saxons (now used as the arms of Essex). The ancient arms of the Leather-sellers' Company of London, which no doubt had much to do with the control and development of Hornchurch's trade in leather, are shown in the left-hand corner, and opposite these are the arms of the noble French family of De Menthon, to which St. Bernard of Savoy (see p. 59), belonged. The seal of the Manor or Liberty of Havering (with the legendary ring shown in the exergue) is portrayed, and also the arms of four ancient families who, as mentioned in the text, were connected with Hornchurch—the families of Legatt, Ayloffe, Withering of Nelmes, and Prujean. The bull's head, which is the unique decoration of the east end of the parish church, is given the place of honour. The two figures represent a Danish chieftain holding a drinking horn, and a monk or friar as representative of Hornchurch Priory. The significance of these figures is explained by the allusions under the heading " How Hornchurch got its name " (p. 61).

Photo]　　　　　　　　　　　　　　　　　　　　　　[*Ernest Milner.*

ST. ANDREW'S CHURCH.

YE OLDE VILLAGE
OF
HORNCHURCH

being an illustrated historical Handbook of the Village and Parish of Hornchurch.

BY
CHARLES THOMAS PERFECT

IAN HENRY PUBLICATIONS

First published in 1917 by
Benham and Company, Limited

Reprinted, with a number of extra illustrations, 1975

Reprinted 1977, 1982, 2005

© Ian Henry Publications, Ltd., 1975, 2005

ISBN 0 86025 540 9

Published by
Ian Henry Publications, Ltd.
20 Park Drive, Romford, Essex RM1 4LH
and printed by
L.P.P.S Ltd.
128 Northampton Road, Wellingborough
Nortamptonshire NN8 3PJ

PREFACE.

IT was recently my intention to publish a History of Hornchurch, on which I have been engaged for several years, but war prices and conditions have made the production of that work in its entirety impossible at the present time. In these circumstances I have compiled from my notes the present small volume, which I venture to publish in the hope that it will meet a repeatedly expressed desire—not only from residents, but from visitors and New Zealanders—for a book on the history of our ancient village.

In writing it I have not been concerned to set out in chronological order a record of ancient local history, but my object has rather been to put together some of the most interesting facts and incidents connected with the village of Hornchurch and its inhabitants, not only in the long past, but in the immediate past and in the present. It has been my endeavour to put such incidents into what I hope may be considered a concise and convenient book of reference. I have given considerable attention to the more recent events surrounding our village life, and, if it should be thought that some of the incidents narrated appear to be of a common-place order, it must be borne in mind that future generations may be as greatly interested in them, as we are to-day in the happenings of a few centuries ago.

I am greatly indebted to Major A. B. Bamford for putting at my disposal his valuable MSS. relating to the Royal Liberty of Havering, and for his drawing of Edward the Confessor ; to Mr. W. Gurney Benham for the beautiful cover design for the book, and for the assistance and advice he has so readily given me in the production of this work ; and to Mrs. Fraser-Parkes, Mr. F. Ford, Mr. Fred Gandon, Mr. Frank Luff,

Mr. Ernest Milner, Mr. Bursall Tonge, and Mr. W. P. Wrack for the photographs reproduced in these pages.

I wish to express my obligation and thanks to the Rev. Herbert Dale, M.A., for allowing me access to the Church Registers, for the loan of various old documents, and for his helpfulness in many other ways ; to Mr. J. R. Robertson for permitting me to peruse his unique collection of village records ; and to Mr. William C. Allen for the assistance he has afforded me in connection with parish statistics, etc. My thanks are also due to that large number of parishioners, most of them old inhabitants, who have helped me with their memories of the past, more especially Mr. and Mrs. C. H. Baker, Mr. E. G. Bratchell, Mr. Isaac Dear, Mr. Walter Dendy, Mr. George Dockrill, Mr. and Mrs. Robert Dockrill, Mr. G. Franklin, Mr. F. W. Franklin, Mr. T. Howard, and Mr. T. W. Wedlake.

For the rest I have consulted most of the recognised authorities on the history of Essex, including Morant, Ogbourne, White, Wright, Coller, Page, the Victoria County Histories, etc., and while gleaning from all of them many interesting details, I have from none derived so much assistance as from Mr. George Terry's " Memories of Old Romford."

The writing of this little volume has afforded me a great deal of pleasure, and, although conscious of many defects in its compilation, I am hopeful that what I have recorded will create among my fellow parishioners an even greater interest than they have hitherto felt in our ancient village.

CHARLES T. PERFECT.

" Weylands," Hornchurch, Essex.

September, 1917.

HORNCHURCH.

HORNCHURCH abounds in historical associations. While it is my intention to write more particularly of that Hornchurch which we know to-day, and which centres in the old village and its more recent extensions represented by the Emerson Park and Great Nelmes Estates, it will be neither possible nor desirable to separate the ancient history of the parish from that wider area known as the Royal Liberty of Havering, which, though now split up into the three distinct parishes of Romford, Havering and Hornchurch, was formerly one civil and ecclesiastical parish, viz., Hornchurch.*

But, although the Hornchurch of long ago has had so much taken from it, it is still of very considerable proportions, its population, at the last census in 1911, being given as 9,462. We, who live in " Our Village," often wonder where such a population is housed, but the apparent mystery is solved when it is explained that the parish is about 6⅛ miles long from north to south, and 2½ miles wide from east to west, that its present boundaries extend as far south as the river Thames, and, stretching northwards, take in part of what is known as South Romford ; that it is bounded on the east by the Ingrebourne, and on the west by the Rom (or Beam) River, and that its area includes South Hornchurch, North-west Hornchurch, Harold Wood and Ardleigh Green, as well as the actual village. Notwithstanding all this, modern Hornchurch folk have some difficulty in realizing that they are living on the banks of the Thames.

The parish, which formerly had two divisions, Northend and Southend, is now divided into four

*In Morant's *History of Essex* (1768, Hornchurch is thus referred to :— " Having surveyed the several Manors within the Liberty of Havering, we come now to consider it as a Parish, for, within these large bounds, it contains only one Parish called Horn-church."

I

Photo, Fred Gandon.] [*By permission of Luffs, Hornchurch.*

OLD HOUSES AT THE WESTERN END OF HIGH STREET.

Wards, viz.:—The Village Ward, North-west Ward, South Ward, and Harold Wood Ward. Its area is 6,773 acres of land and ten of water, and its rateable value in March, 1916, was £60,216.

While it has its own Parish Council and a Parochial Committee, it forms part of the Romford Rural District Council, which covers an area of 47,652 acres, and includes the parishes of Upminster, Hornchurch, Cranham, Wennington, Great Warley, Havering, Noak Hill, Dagenham and Rainham.

From 1885 to 1917, Hornchurch was in the Romford Parliamentary Division, the largest in the Kingdom, with an electorate in 1916 of 62,878, its member being Sir John H. Bethell, Bart., who has sat for the constituency since 1906, in the Liberal and Radical interests.

Hornchurch is in the Romford Petty Sessional Division, Poor Law Union, Rural District and County Court Circuit.

The soil generally is light, and the subsoil gravel. The village is situated in one of the prettiest parts of Essex, about 13 miles from London on the London, Tilbury and Southend Section of the Midland Railway. In a county which is erroneously said to be flat, it is on fairly high ground, the altitude on the top of the hill on which St. Andrew's church stands being given in the Ordnance map as 118 feet above sea level.

When I first saw our village High Street, with its ancient gabled houses, projecting stories, dormer windows, and curiously carved and moulded fronts, it was still to a large extent unspoiled by modern "improvements," and it can readily be imagined that when that picturesque street, with its cobbled sidewalks, and North Street, Church Hill, Billet Lane, Suttons Lane and Wingletye Lane, with the beautiful old church on the hill-top, and the ancient windmill at the far end of the Dell, together with the outlying farmsteads, comprised the whole of the village (as distinct from the parish), the inhabitants were well content with their pleasant surroundings. Also they may have been proud of their village from the commercial point of view; for industries of some note have been carried on here in times past.

3

The Leather Dressing Industry.

As far back as the 12th century, a very considerable trade was done here in currying and leather dressing, and the main street was appropriately called Pell or Pelt Street, owing to the large number of Fellmongers, Skinners and Tanners who carried on their business there. In those days leather was very largely used in the making of men's clothes, and it will, therefore, be seen that an industry such as that which flourished in Pell Street—entirely connected with the leather trade—was one of the staple industries of the day. It was, moreover, for the facilitating of that trade that the privilege of holding a market was first granted to the town of Romford in the reign of Henry III., and doubtless Hornchurch sent most of its wares into that town, which appears to have been quite famous for its leathern breeches.

The importance of this village industry was such that it was supposed by one authority that Hornchurch owes the derivation of its name to it. The Rev. W. Pallin, in his " Stifford and its Neighbourhood," says :— " It is conjectured that Horn-church took its name from the colony of curriers settled there, whose sign, ' a pair of horns,' still ornaments the east wall of the church."*

I think it quite likely that this conjecture was as near the truth as any, and for this reason :—In a Royal Charter of Henry II. the Church is described as the Church of Havering (Ecclesia de Havering), but in a later Charter, in 1253, granted by Henry III., it is for the first time designated " Cornutum Monasterium," or Horned Monastery. Now, seeing that in 1247 that same Monarch granted Romford its market for the primary purpose of carrying on its leather trade, it may well be that our village had so firmly established its industry of leather dressing for supplying that market, that its sign of a pair of horns was generally well known when the Charter of 1253 was made to the church, and to associate its trade emblem with the only church then standing within that wide area known as Havering appears to me quite natural and reasonable.

*The various assumed derivations of the name of Hornchurch will be found on page 61.

4

This again is only supposition, and no one knows to this day how or why our village got its name of Hornchurch, (or Hornchirche, as it was later described in English in a further Charter in the reign of Edward

OLD DOORWAY, MR. A. FERGUSON'S HOUSE, NORTH STREET.

III.), or how it came about that the Bull's Head and Horns appear at the east end of the church.

The leather dressing industry continued in a more

or less flourishing condition in our village for about six centuries. It is not known when it began to wane, but it ceased altogether, as far as tanning was concerned, about 70 years ago, though as recently as the year 1870 a Mr. Fry was carrying on the business of a Fellmonger at the premises now occupied by Mr. A. Ferguson in North Street. Up to about the year 1846, there were tanyards in High Street at the back of what is now Messrs. Page, Calnan and Co.'s Yard, and also in a yard off the High Street at the rear of the position on which the Bank Buildings now stand. Messrs. Bright and Beardwell had their business there, and they also had Fellmongers' pits at the rear of the King's Head Inn, on the spot which is now the Quoit Ground. They were the last firm of Tanners in Hornchurch.

No mention is made of any Tannery in a list of Hornchurch traders published in 1848.

FAIRKYTES FOUNDRY.

It was not only in the leather dressing industry that Hornchurch was famous in the past ; it held quite a conspicuous position in the agricultural world for over a century, owing to its manufactures of agricultural implements.

In the year 1784 there came to Hornchurch two brothers, Thomas and Robert Wedlake, who established and made famous Fairkytes Foundry in Billet Lane.

Many people doubtless wonder how it is that the little cottage in Billet Lane, with its heavy door so artistically studded with big nails, came to be there, and why there hang at the side of it those large gates, which look so imposing beside so small a house. Those were the gates leading to Fairkytes Foundry, which originally stood in what is now Mr. J. R. Robertson's meadow, and the little cottage was the foundry office.

In those days the term " engineer " had not the general application that it has now-a-days, and the Wedlakes described themselves as millwrights. Thomas

6

was the head of the firm and the business man, and
Robert the mechanic, and the combination worked so
well that in course of time they became famous all over
the country as agricultural implement makers and
patentees. Robert Wedlake invented the double-action
haymaking machine, which is largely in use at the present
time. In its palmiest days a dozen forges were kept
continually at work at the foundry, and from 80 to 90
hands were employed there all the year round.

Photo]   [*Frank Luff.*

THE OLD FOUNDRY COTTAGE, BILLET LANE.

The importance of Fairkytes Foundry and its manufactures is indicated by the presentation of a valuable
piece of plate by the agriculturists of the Eastern
Counties to Mr. Thomas Wedlake at the White Hart,
Romford, on the 7th August, 1833, to express their
indebtedness to him for his many inventions and
improvements of agricultural implements. The pre-

sentation took the form of a silver tea urn, weighing
160 ounces, which bore the inscription :—

Presented to Mr. Thomas Wedlake,
Ironfounder of Hornchurch in Essex,
By the landlords and yeomanry, patrons of agriculture,
and practical farmers of the Eastern Counties,
As a token of their esteem for his assiduity and skill,
evinced by his numerous inventions and improvements of
Agricultural Implements. At the Market Table, White Hart
Inn, Romford. Christopher Tower, of Weald Hall, Esq., M.P.,
in the chair, August 7, 1833.

It is possible to form some idea of the general appreciation in which Mr. Wedlake and his inventions were held, when we learn that the subscriptions, with but few exceptions, were limited to 2s 6d. from each individual.

On the death of Mr. Thomas Wedlake, his widow and son-in-law carried on the original business under the style of Mary Wedlake and Co., and Mr. Robert Wedlake and a Mr. Thompson started in opposition in the High Street, next the " Bull Inn," as Wedlake and Thompson, Union Foundry. The latter business was purchased by Mr. Richard Dendy, who, in 1848, entered into partnership with Mr. Thomas W. Wedlake, son of Mr. Robert Wedlake, who is now our oldest male inhabitant, having been born in the village on November 17, 1828. For many years he filled the office of People's Warden at the Parish Church.

In later years Mr. Walter Dendy took his father's place in the Union Foundry, and in 1902 the business was transferred to Barking under the name of the London Scottish Foundry.

The present engineering works in North Street are carried on by Mr. T. W. Wedlake and his sons, Robert and Sidney, under the style of Thos. W. Wedlake and Co.

THE OLD HORNCHURCH BREWERY.

It is not without reason that the brewery on Church Hill bears the name of the Old Hornchurch Brewery, for it is nearly 130 years since it was established on the site of the present building. It was in 1789 that one John Woodfine laid the foundation of a business, which, after being carried on by three successive generations of his family, was purchased in 1874 by Messrs. Henry and Benjamin Holmes : from them it passed in 1889 to Mr. Charles Dagnall, who converted it into a limited liability company, under the style of the Old Horn-church Brewery Company, Limited. This venture, however, did not prove successful, and after a few years the company went into liquidation. In June, 1892, Mr. Philip P. Conron purchased it from the Official Receiver, and at his death in 1894, his two sons, Philip S. Conron and Stanislaus R. Conron, succeeded him. The first named died in 1897, and since then the management has devolved upon Mr. S. R. Conron.

THE POTTERY AND BRICK AND TILE WORKS.

On entering the village from the Hornchurch Road, after passing over Raven's Bridge, under which trickles a small tributary of the Rom, one reaches the Red House, at the top of the slight incline, almost im-mediately opposite Grey Towers entrance, At the rear of Red House are the remains of what was once a flourishing pottery and brick and tile works. The soil at this spot was evidently suitable for that industry, as a large area of it has been excavated to a considerable depth. These works were, until recently, carried on by Mr. Stone, and were originally established there about 200 years ago. Mr. Charles Cove is given in *White's Essex* as the proprietor in 1848, and it is interesting to know that the larger of the two jugs shown on page 78 and dated 1815, was made at these works.

Agriculture.

Apart from the industries mentioned, Hornchurch, owing to its remarkably fertile soil, has always been largely agricultural. In July 1812, a return was made to Parliament which gave the following particulars :—

Inhabited houses	286
Uninhabited houses	8
Families chiefly employed in Agriculture	197 ⎫
Families employed in trade and manufacture..	80 ⎬ 319
All other families not comprised in the preceding classes	42 ⎭
Population :—Males	842
Females	723
	1567

9

It will be seen from this that nearly two-thirds of the total population must at that time have been employed in agricultural pursuits. Thirty-six years later, *White's Essex* gives a list of no less than 23 Hornchurch farmers, and even at the present day it may still be said that the chief industry of Hornchurch remains on the soil. Here may be seen some of the finest grain crops in the kingdom, and the sight of the

Photo]   [*W. P. Wrack.*

OLD GABLED HOUSES, HIGH STREET.

golden corn in August, when the fields are ripe for the harvest, is a thing of beauty, and worth coming many miles to see.

All the year round market gardening on a large scale is carried on, and every night heavy waggons, laden with seasonable field produce, rumble through the old village streets on their way to the London markets.

10

Village Trading.

The shopkeeping community of Hornchurch at the present time does not appear to be on the up-grade, and when compared with 70 years ago the number of tradesmen carrying on business in the village would appear to suffer by way of comparison. At that time there were 7 Bakers, 6 Butchers, 5 Grocers, 5 Drapers and Tailors, 2 Hairdressers, 6 Boot and Shoe Makers, 4 Carpenters, 3 Blacksmiths, 2 Ironfounders, and 17 Public Houses and Beerhouses.

Among the old Hornchurch business names in those days may be mentioned Aldous, Cressy, Dendy, Dockrill, Franklyn, Frost, Fry, Grout, Manning, Playle, Sibthorp, Tyler, and Wedlake.

At the end of the list of tradesmen is the following quaint announcement :—

Post Office at W. Frost's. Letters from Romford daily. Carriers to London Tuesday and Friday. Peter Smith and George Rigten.

THE OLD WINDMILL AND MILLFIELD.

Before the introduction of steam grinding machinery, the Windmill was of paramount importance in our village life, and the occupation of the miller one of the most necessary and useful to the community.

I have been unable to trace the exact date when the Windmill first reared its mighty arms to the four winds of heaven. That it was there in the time of James I. seems to be certain, for John Legat, who was living at Hornchurch Hall in 1607, and dated his will from there, bequeathed* the Mill to his son Thomas. This proves beyond dispute that it was in existence quite early in the 17th century, and in all probability it was standing at the far end of the Dell very many years before that.

The next earliest record of the occupancy of the Mill, that I have been able to obtain, dates from the early part of the 19th century, when for some years prior to 1822 the Mill was leased to a Mr. Mason ; but in the year named Mr. John Bearblock, who lived at Hornchurch

* This would mean his rights as lessee only, as the Mill was included in the property owned by New College, Oxford.

II

From a photo in possession of Mr. Thomas Howard.

THE WINDMILL.

Bared to the winds of heaven, my giant arms
  Welcome the raging storm, the winter's chill.
These more I love than summer's gentle charms.
  Give me the hurricane my sails to fill !

C. T. PERFECT.

Hall, came into possession, and carried on the business until about the year 1846, when a new tenant, Mr. Richard Stevens, became the occupier. After a period of something like four years, another change took place, Mr. Bearblock again becoming the lessee, and he was followed in 1852 by Mr. John Mitchell, who in the year 1861 relinquished his interest in the business in favour of his son Edward. He, upon coming into occupation, added a separate steam mill as an adjunct to the windmill. In 1897 Mr. Thomas C. Howard (who had acted as manager to Mr. E. Mitchell) and his brother, Mr. George E. Howard, became joint lessees, and worked the mills until 1912, since when no milling has been carried

Photo]   *[C. T. Perfect.*
THE WINDMILL AND MILL COTTAGE.

on, the old windmill having ceased to operate, by reason of the sails and other important parts of the structure having become so unsafe as to preclude all possibility of its working in its present condition.

The steam mill building still stands, but this was dismantled of its machinery some few years ago, and the whole plant disposed of.

It is worthy of note that the name of Howard has been associated with the Windmill, and the old-world thatched cottage adjacent, for over 90 years, the late Mr. Thomas Howard, father of the present tenants, having come to Hornchurch in 1822 to enter the service of Mr. Bearblock, and subsequently following on with that gentleman's successors.

Millfield, or the Dell, is perhaps *the* beauty spot of Hornchurch, and I doubt if a much prettier sight can be seen anywhere within the borders of the county. A lovely grassy dell, beautifully wooded, with the ancient church at one end, and the old mill at the other, is a picture which has gladdened the heart of many an artist and photographer, and there are probably few places in rural Essex which have been painted and " snap-shotted " oftener than this one-time gravel pit.

Wrestling for the Boar's Head.

The Millfield was celebrated for the ancient custom of wrestling for a Boar's Head on Christmas Day. There seems to be no reliable record as to when this quaint custom had its beginning, but in the *Essex Review* for April, 1890, it is referred to in the following passage from *Hone's Every day Book*, 1826 :—

" On Christmas Day the following custom has been observed from time immemorial. The Lessee of the Tythes, which belong to New College, Oxford, supplies a Boar's Head, dressed and garnished with bay leaves, etc. In the afternoon it is carried in procession into the Millfield adjoining the Churchyard, where it is wrestled for, and it is afterwards feasted upon at one of the public houses by the rustic conqueror and his friends, with all the merriment peculiar to the season."

One of our oldest inhabitants, who witnessed many of the bouts for the Boar's Head, tells us that it was cooked at Hornchurch Hall, where the first slice was always cut off. It was then brought into the Millfield on a pitchfork, bedecked with ribbons and holly, and with an orange in its mouth. Often as many as twenty wrestlers competed for the prize.

In later years the wrestling match was between the men of Hornchurch and Romford, but, owing to its developing into rather a rowdy affair, the residents of Hornchurch petitioned for its discontinuance, and it was accordingly done away with. On the Christmas

afternoon of 1868 the Boar's Head was competed for
for the last time. Mr. Walter Dendy has been able to
fix the date of this, and he himself saw the procession
pass down the High Street on that occasion.

The Great Prize Fight.

In the Millfield also took place the famous prize-fight
mentioned in Conan Doyle's novel, " Rodney Stone,"
between Mendoza the Jew and Jackson. Mendoza was
one of the most celebrated professional prize fighters of
his day, and Jackson a gentleman boxer well-known
in the highest circles of society, and a man greatly
esteemed for many sterling qualities. The fight is
thus described in *Pugilistica,* vol. 1 (Henry Downes
Miles) :—

" Jackson's next contest was one of the greatest interest
to the pugilistic world. The victories of Mendoza had placed
him on a pinnacle of fame, and the attempt to defeat the conqueror of Sam Martin, of Humphries (twice) and Bill Warr
(twice), to say nothing of minor boxers, was viewed as indeed
a bold flight of young ambition. On April 15th, 1795, the men
met at Hornchurch in Essex, for a stake of 200 guineas aside.

A 24-feet stage was erected in a most advantageous hollow,
which accommodated upwards of 3,000 spectators, and was so
excellently adapted that no one could claim a superiority of
situation. All the eminent patrons and amateurs were present :
the Duke of Hamilton, Lord Delaval, Sir John Phillipson, Mr.
Clark, Mr. Bullock, Mr. Lee, Mr. Fawcett, etc., and among the
pugilists of note were Jackling, Will Warr and Joe Warr, George
the Brewer, Tom Tyne, Fearby (the young Ruffian), &c.

At one o'clock Mendoza mounted the spot of combat, accom-
panied by his second, Harry Lea, and Symonds (the old Ruffian)
as his bottle holder. Jackson immediately followed, with Tom
Johnson as his second, and Woods, the coachman, for his bottle
holder. The chosen umpires were Mr. Alexander and Mr. Allen.

They each politely bowed to the people, and were received
with general acclamations. About five minutes after one
o'clock, they, as usual, saluted each other by shaking hands,
and immediately set-to. Bets 5 to 4 on Mendoza."

The fight was decided in nine rounds, and at the end
of the seventh round the odds had changed to 2 to 1
on Jackson.

The 9th round is thus described :—

" This was the last round. Jackson manifestly displayed
astonishing advantage ; he several times struck his adversary,

when he (Mendoza) fell quite exhausted and gave in. The battle only lasted $10\frac{1}{2}$ minutes, and was acknowledged by every spectator to be the hardest contested that ever was fought in so short a time. Jackson was very little hurt, leaped from the stage with great agility, but Mendoza was quite cut up."

John Jackson died on October 7, 1845. His remains rest beneath a handsome monument in Brompton Cemetery, erected by " several noblemen and gentlemen to record their admiration of one whose excellence of heart and incorruptible worth endeared him to all who knew him."

Cockfighting.

In the 18th century the Millfield was one of the most noted cockpits around London, and many battles were fought there. I am able to reproduce press notices of two of these, which took place in the year 1769, but unfortunately the exact dates are not given :—

* 1769, COCKFIGHTING.—At Hornchurch in Essex last week Mr. Crump beat Lord Waltham by many bouts ahead ; Champ Feeder for Mr. Crump, and Dorrill of Chelmsford for Lord Waltham.

* 1769. COCKFIGHTING :—The third annual Cock Match between the Gentlemen of London and the Gentlemen of Essex was fought at Hornchurch on Monday, Tuesday and Wednesday last. There were 36 bouts in the main, and 19 Byes, out of which the Essex Gentlemen won 36 bouts in the main and 11 Byes.

POPULATION AND RATEABLE VALUE.

YEAR.	POPULATION.	YEAR	POPULATION.
1801	1331	1861	2227
1811	1656	1871	2476
1821	1938	1881	2824
1831	2186	1891	3841
1841	2399	1901	6402
1851	2378	1911	9462

				GROSS ESTIMATED RENTAL. £	RATEABLE VALUE. £
1875	..	..	..	21730	18613
1880	..	..	..	25043	21032
1885	..	..	..	24789	20210

*The above notices were taken from some cuttings from 1769 newspapers, but the name or names of the papers and the exact dates are missing. C.T.P.

				GROSS ESTIMATED RENTAL. £	RATEABLE VALUE. £
1890	..	..	..	29272	23409
1895	..	..	..	32736	26220
1900	..	..	..	43540	34894
1905	..	..	..	57445	45307
1910	..	..	..	65088	52465
1915	..	..	..	74927	59259
1916	..	..	..	76092	60216

In 1916 there were 2,377 dwelling houses in Hornchurch.

*In the time of Edward IV. (1547–1553) the following is the description given of Hornchurch and its population :—

" The said town of Hornchurch is a populous town, having six hundred of howselinget people and more."

THE OLD VILLAGE AND ITS HOUSES.

Until the year 1877, an **Annual Fair** was held in Hornchurch Village on Whit Monday. This was quite on old-time lines, booths being erected in the High Street, where could be bought the old fashioned fairings, including the famous gilded gingerbread in all its attractive and fantastic shapes and designs. The merry-go-round was always placed in the middle of the crossroads at the High Street end of the Billet Lane, close by what was known as the Workhouse Pond.

In these days when one grumbles at the regularity of the arrival of the demands for the quarterly Water Rate, it is apt to be forgotten that water was not always conveyed through pipes to our houses, and there served through taps to wherever convenience may demand, and it is perhaps only known to a few of the oldest inhabitants that a public or semi-public well once existed at the rear of what is now " Luccombe," Mr. C. H. Baker's residence in Sutton's Lane. The spot was known as **Soane's Well Piece,** and one halfpenny was charged by the owner for every pail of water drawn from the well. That well is still in existence.

At the rear of **Chain House,** Mr. Drake's residence

* Ogborne's *Essex.*
† Communicants.

17

in the High Street, was another well of a similar kind, in a small field, known as Jimmy Stevens' Orchard. The water from that well was supposed to be free to all comers, but the said Jimmy, who was a baker by trade, and owned the well, was a cute old chap, for it is said that preferential treatment was given to his customers, and that if you did not happen to be one of those fortunate individuals, you had to pass on to " Soane's Well " and pay your ha'penny.

Photo] [*Richard Dendy*.
HIGH STREET END OF BILLET LANE 50 YEARS AGO
SHOWING THE OLD WORKHOUSE POND.

Mason's Well.—At the back of the Windmill, or rather in the field to the south of it, is a spring of most excellent water, and many years ago a Waterloo veteran, named Mason, used to add to his small military pension by drawing water from the spring, and hawking it round at a ha'penny a pail. Mason was a giant, and stood 6 feet 4 inches. He was quite a village celebrity

Photo]

THE COTTAGE, NORTH STREET.

[Frank Luff.

n those days, and with his great height and exceedingly gruff voice, was a terror to all the small boys of the neighbourhood. He lived at one time in that tiny house on Church Hill, next the chemist's shop on the west side, which was then known as **Punch's Castle**, and rumour has it that he was so tall, and his bedroom so small, that he slept with his feet out of the front window. Rumour, however, is not always a truth-teller, and Mason probably only cooled his feet in that way during the summer months.

The old houses and shops of the High Street, North Street, and Church Hill, with the Manor Houses, and some few of the larger ancient houses and farmsteads in close proximity, will always be looked upon as the **Old Village,** as distinct from that more modern Horn-church which has sprung up during recent years, par-ticularly since Emerson Park opened out as a residential estate in 1895.

This old village may generally be described as of the 17th century, and many of the shops and small houses are of that period, as are also the **White House,** occupied by Mr. T. W. Wedlake, and formerly known as Grosvenor House, and **" The Cottage "** in North Street, occupied in 1917 by Nurses of the New Zealand Contingent Hospital. The **" Bull Inn,"** the **" Crick-eters "** and the **" King's Head "*** date back to a similar period, the latter inn being one of the old coach-ing houses.

The carving on the most beautiful specimen of all the old overhanging fronts, viz., that opposite Billet Lane, is late 16th century, or early 17th century work.†

The present **" Chequers Inn "** on Butts Green replaced about 18 years ago an old hostel of the same name, with red tiled roof and of a style of architecture in keeping with the other ancient houses of the village.

The old flat timber **Archway in the High Street,**

* This house is referred to in the Parish Registers in the following curious entry : —
   " At the Vestry held in the usual place on the 10th day of November
   " 1801. Mr. John Higgs', Overseer of the Poor paid as follows :—
   " £85 6s 7d.
   " This Vestry is adjourned to the King's Head. John Thompson, Vestry
   " Clerk."
† This carving is said to have come from the Parish Church when restored.

and the house adjoining it on the east side (erroneously called, by some, the Manor House) are undoubtedly of the 16th century. This old archway takes one back to the days when highwaymen infested the roads, and made travelling by coach a somewhat hazardous busi-

THE OLD ARCHWAY, HIGH STREET.

ness. A notorious character, who went under the name of Jimmy Wood, and was said to be the illegitimate son of the wife of a butcher living in Hornchurch, held up the Royal Mail Coach one dark night on the high road between Hare Street and Brentwood. He got plugged with a bullet, but was not mortally injured, for he managed to find his way back to an old barn at the bottom of the yard under the old archway in High Street, and there he hid under the straw while his mother nursed him back to health, and by that means was able to elude the vigilance of the preventive men, who had a warrant for his arrest. After he recovered from his wound he got clean away, but it is said that he was ultimately captured, and came to an untimely end.

Mr. Robert Wedlake, one of the founders of the Fairkytes Foundry, knew this highwayman, and I give the tale as it was told by him to his son, Mr. T. W. Wedlake.

The present **White Hart Hotel** is built on the site of a house which was destroyed by fire on the night of November 7th, 1872. The old White Hart was reputed to be many centuries old, and was said to be the most picturesque building in the village. It had gables and an overhanging front. A notable feature of this quaint old hoseltry was a large sundial on its main chimney stack.

Billet Lane takes its name from the public house named the " **Crooked Billet,**"* which stood on the spot now occupied by the house called " **The Billet.**" The present building is part of a modern house which replaced the original building, which was of some antiquity, being about 300 years old when it was pulled down. It was a gabled house with dormer windows and a thatched roof, and was placed farther back from the road than the present house. The " Crooked Billet " was closed about 50 years ago.

The old **Harrow Inn,** shewn on the opposite page, was pulled down in 1894, and the present house, in Hornchurch Road, was built on the site. This ancient inn, with its thatched roof and wooded front, was typical of many of the old public houses in the neighbourhood, which have now either been replaced by more modern buildings, or have altogether ceased to exist.

* The following is from a newspaper of 1831 (exact date missing) : —" Died lately Mr. John Clift, 50 years landlord of the Crooked Billet, Hornchurch."

22

THE OLD HARROW INN.

Mrs. Dodd, the present landlady of the Harrow, lived for some years in the old Harrow, and has been associated with the two houses for over 28 years.

Cage Row is the curious name given to the small row of old cottages in North Street by the side of the Baptist Church, and the reason it was so called is that immediately opposite there once stood the Village Lockup, which was appropriately known as **" The Cage."** It was a small building capable of accommodating only two or three persons, and was built right over the pathway and abutted on to the road. Prisoners were lodged there for the night when arrested in, or near, the village, and in the morning were conveyed to the nearest jail.

That the Cage was in existence in 1679 is proved by the following quaint entry in the Overseers' Account book for that year :—

	s.	d.
For a coffin for a broom* man yt dyed in ye Cage ..	8	o
For an old blankett for ye same man	2	o
For beer for ye men yt carried him to buriall ..	3	o
For stripping ye same man	1	o
To Mr. Wells double duties for ye said Buriall ..	2	8
For a journey to ye Justice to give oath about the Buryall of ye broom man abovesd	2	o

The Cage was removed about sixty years ago.

The Old Workhouse was at the High Street corner of Billet Lane, and formed part, or the whole, of the small block of buildings now comprising **Pennant's Almshouses** and the tailor's shop and cottage at the extreme corner. Although the whole of this property was originally left by Pierce† Pennant for Almshouses, it is recorded that in the year 1720 a Workhouse was erected there, and remained in use until the formation of the Union in 1834, and probably for some time after that date. It does not appear how it came about that the Almshouses were superseded, or replaced, by the Workhouse. As, however, the same local authority which would control the Workhouse (or Poor House) before the Poor Law Amendment Act, 1834, came in force, would, in all probability, be the same

* A broom man was a man who went about the country hawking brooms.
+ See al o page 106, under Charities.

24

as that which controlled the charities, viz., the Vicar, Churchwardens and Overseers, it is quite possible that they considered that the purposes of the Charity was at that period served by what was then more generally known as the Poor House.

William Pennant, of London, in his Will, dated May 4th, 1607, mentions the Almshouses in the following

Photo]   *[W. P. Wrack*

CORNER OF HIGH STREET AND NORTH STREET, SHOWING THE OLD "BRITANNIA" AND CAGE ROW.

terms :—" The Poore House in Hornchurch which my uncle did give to the Towne."

I have extracted a few entries from the Parish Registers directly concerning the Workhouse. These are not only curious in their wording, but some of them give an idea of the price of provisions, etc., which will be found interesting, especially by way of comparison in these days of war-time prices :—

June 7, 1725 :—To Mr. Wood to be layd out for ye clothing for ye Poor in ye Workhouse £6 12s. 9d.

April 1764 :—Paid for teaching the Workhouse children 3 qrs. of a year £4 10s.

April 1764 :—For a year's rent of a Schoolroom due at Easter, 10s.

April 1772 :—Towards a Schoolroom, and pens, ink and paper, 3s.

May 2nd, 1785 :—To changing warming pan, 5s.

May 2nd, 1785 :—67 lbs. Cheese for Workhouse 22s. 4d.

May 2nd, 1785 :—14 lbs. Sope for Workhouse, 8s.

January 8, 1788 :—Gave the Poor in the House for Xmas Box 5s. 6d.

September 3, 1792 :—Paid Schroffill Nokes for mending the Workhouse Copper, 7s. 9d.

April 17, 1795 :—Paid to Mrs. Rigby for a Sheep wt. 8st. 1lb., 20s.

The following is from a newspaper cutting of 1835 :—

Longevity :—" There are at this time in Hornchurch Workhouse, eight men whose united ages amount to 634 years ; also five women, whose ages amount to 412 years, the youngest of whom is 81 years."

ABBS CROSS.

Nearly opposite the entrance to Grey Towers are the cross roads known as ABBS CROSS. This spot would appear to be named after St. Ebba, the name being corrupted to St. Abbs. St. Ebba founded a monastery, of which she became Abbess at St. Abbs, East Berwick, Scotland, in the 7th century (about A.D. 683). Her name day in the calendar is August 25. Exactly how Abbs Cross came by its name is lost in antiquity, but there is little doubt that there is some connection between that early Saint and the cross-roads at the western end of our village High Street.

THE MANOR HOUSES.

Of the seventeen Manor Houses comprised in the Royal Liberty of Havering, four were in the immediate vicinity of the village, viz. :—Nelmes, Hornchurch Hall, Suttons and Lees Gardens.

The Manor of Nelmes.

Nelmes was the most noted of these four Manors

NELMES.

Part of the beautiful old mansion, now owned and occupied by Mr. Alfred Barber, was earlier than the time of Elizabeth, and in all probability this house was enlarged or considerably altered by a member of the Roche family during her reign. Sir William Roche, who was Lord Mayor of London in 1540, died possessed of Nelmes in 1549, but was buried in London. He was succeeded by his son John, and he by his son Thomas, who is later described as of the Manor of " Gooses."

It is not known when the Roche family parted with Nelmes, but *Wright* tells us that Robert Harvey died there in 1608 and that he left it to his son John. The same authority also states that " in 1627 Robert Naunton, Esq. was Lord of this Manor, which soon after seems to have had several parcels of land taken from it and purchased by different persons, and what remained of it became the property of Sir Thomas Webster, Bart., of Copped Hall and Battle Abbey in Sussex, and of his son Godfrey Webster, Esq."

Ogborne gives Charles Pratt, Esq., as having died at Nelmes on February 5th, 1624.

In the middle of the 17th century Thomas Witheringe, who was Postmaster General to Charles I, was living there. He died on his way to Church on Sunday morning, September 28th, 1651, and his alabaster mural monument with a long inscription can be seen in St. Andrew's Church. His son Thomas, who he hoped would succeed him in his office, died young, as did also his daughter Dorothy. His nephew, William Witheringe, succeeded to his office, and, as heir to his uncle, occupied Nelmes. He was living there in 1661, for Edward Slaney, of Hornchurch, in his Will dated May 8th of that year, says :—" I give to William Witheringe, of Nelmes, Esq., £700 out of which to pay legacies, etc., etc."

The Harding-Newmans were living in Hornchurch in the latter part of the 18th century, and at least three generations of the family resided at Nelmes. They largely identified themselves with foxhunting, as will be seen from the following extract from the *Victoria County History of Essex*, vol. II. The reference

to Romney's famous picture *The Pink Boy* in this
connection is also of considerable interest :—

"On the southern side of the county Mr. William Russell, of
'Stubbers,' near Romford, had a famous pack of foxhounds
in the 18th century. He was followed by Mr. Richard Newman
Harding Newman, of Nelmes, near Hornchurch. This gentle-

OLD GOTHIC GATEWAY, NELMES.

man came of an old Essex family, his grandfather, Richard
Newman, having been High Sheriff of the county in 1762.
Though resident outside the present limits of the 'Essex'
country, he extended his operations into it, having kennels at
Broomfield near Chelmsford, and at Navestock; and, as we
are told that Mr. Conyers, on purchasing Mr. Newman's hounds,

hunted "the same country," the latter may fairly be regarded as the actual founder of the present Essex Hunt. His portrait, painted by George Romney, and known as *The Pink Boy*, is considered to rival in artistic merit *The Blue Boy* of Gainsborough. The picture is now in the possession of Lord Burton, who has kindly sanctioned its use as an illustration."[*]

In *Wright's History of Essex* (1835), Nelmes is mentioned as the seat of Richard Newman, Esq.

Dr. Thomas Harding Newman[†], who was a Fellow of Magdalen College, Oxford, resided at Nelmes for many years, and during his occupancy he acquired and brought to Nelmes an old oaken Gothic gateway, with a door opening out of it. This is said to have been the original gateway to the old Balliol College, and it is recorded that the three martyrs, Cranmer, Ridley and Latimer, were burnt at the stake " against the ditch of Balliol," opposite to which this gateway originally stood. Dr. Newman died in 1880, and was succeeded in the occupation of Nelmes by his nephew, Benjamin Harding Newman.

Although the house was originally Elizabethan or earlier date, wings were added, or it was partly rebuilt, in the first half of the 17th century, and again either at the end of that century or early in the 18th century, and the present mansion is entirely of that period, the Elizabethan portion having been pulled down. With it disappeared two Elizabethan staircases which were situated to the east of the building. Major A. B. Bamford made a drawing of one of these staircases while they were still in position.

There is a very fine carved oaken staircase at present in the mansion, of the time of Charles I. It is probably one of the best examples of the work of that period in the country.

Of the more recent occupiers of Nelmes were Mr. Harry Holmes, the eldest son of the late Colonel Holmes, and Mr. Louis Sinclair during part of the time the Romford Division was represented by him in Parliament.

Mr. Alfred Barber came into residence at Nelmes in the year 1903.

[*] A print of this picture appears between pages 566-7, *Victoria County History of Essex*, vol. ii.

[†] Dr. Newman was also the owner of the Manor of Mawneys.

The grounds retain their old-world character, and, with the lake and walled garden, and the orchard beyond, form an appropriate setting for the ancient mansion. On the lawn stand two magnificent cedars of Lebanon, one of which is said to be a most perfect specimen of its kind, and amongst the finest in the kingdom. With the exception of these grounds, and a meadow in front of the mansion, the well wooded park of 240 acres is now being developed as a residential

THE STAIRCASE AT NELMES.

estate. If one has to regret that such an historic domain, after many centuries of splendid isolation, has to follow the trend of most of the picturesque and convenient spots near the metropolis, to provide sites for country homes for many of those who have their business in the great City, there is some compensation in the knowledge that the houses which have been built are

of a style of architecture, for the most part, in keeping
with their historic surroundings, and that the owner,
while carefully preserving the coppice and woods on
the estate, has imposed restrictions which render pro-
hibitive the felling of the many fine old trees which
abound there, and which add so much to the beauty
of the landscape, even when broken up by the modern
villa and bungalow.

The Manor of Hornchurch Hall.

The Manor of Hornchurch Hall was granted (together
with the Manor of Suttons) by Henry II. to the Hostel
of St. Bernard de Monte Jovis, and passed, with the
properties belonging to it at Hornchurch, to New
College, Oxford, when William of Wykeham purchased
it from the Brethren of the Hostel. Hornchurch Hall,
which is situated almost opposite St. Andrew's Church,
is, however, not mentioned as a Manor until 1549.

For the first half of the 17th century the Legats
appear to have been living there as the lessees of the
College. The family of Legat was both wealthy and
influential, and Mr. Terry speaks of them as follows :—

" We find no less than twelve generations living in the neighbourhood of Romford, extending over three centuries and a
half, and occupying at one time or another many of the great
houses of the Liberty."

Some of the family were living in Hornchurch in the
16th century, for Thomas Legat, of Dagnams, in his
will, dated 16th January, 1555, mentions William
Legate of Hornchurch, and desires to be buried at
Hornchurch near his father. This wish was complied
with, and is thus recorded in Machyn's Diary :—

" The xii day of January was bered in Essex master Leygett,
justes of pesse, with ii whyt branchys and a dosen of torchys,
and iiii gret tapurs and a gret dolle, and mony mornars, and a
gret dener : and shroyft sonday was ys monyth myne, and ii
dosen stayffs more, and a gret dolle to the pore and a ii dosen
skochyons."

The great grandfather of this Thomas Legat was
High Sheriff of Essex in 1401 and 1408, and his father,
who was buried at Hornchurch, was Lord of the Manor

Photo]

HORNCHURCH HALL.

[Frank Luff.

of Cockerels, and of Gobions, and of a considerable part of Hornchurch.

In 1607 the representative of the Legats living at the Hall was John Legat, who was followed in 1622 by Thomas Legat, and he probably was the last of the Legat family to occupy it.

The Hall then came into the possession of the Thorowgoods, the first of whom—George—died on the 20th January, 1648. He was followed by John Thorowgood, who died in 1668, and was succeeded by George Thorowgood, who died in 1683. He appears to be the last of the family to occupy the Hall, but some members of the family were living in Hornchurch for quite another 100 years after that date.

Joseph Bennett was living at the Hall in 1726, and was followed by Richard Spencer in 1750, to whose memory a beautiful marble memorial by Flaxman is erected on the north wall of the chancel in Hornchurch Church.

In the early part of the 19th century the Hall was in the occupation of the Rev. James Bearblock, M.A., Fellow of King's College, Cambridge. Two generations of the Bearblock family* lived there and identified themselves to a very considerable extent with church and local affairs generally. The Rev. J. Bearblock, who was formerly a master at Eton, acted for some time as Assistant Curate at Upminster Church. He died 1st April, 1841, at the age of 76 years. He had three sons and four daughters, all of whom, with the exception of one son, Peter Esdaile Bearblock, who resided at "Lilliputs," remained unmarried.

In *White's Essex* (1848) appears the following :—

"Walter Bearblock, Esq., of Hornchurch Hall, a neat mansion with tasteful grounds."

John Bearblock, his brother, was joint occupier of the Hall with him, and these three brothers— Peter, Walter and John—were largely instrumental

* The following extract from "The Worthies of Devon" (Sir Thomas Bodley, 1810) has reference to the first of the Bearblocks :—In the year of our Lord 1566, I proceeded Master of Arts, and read for that year, in the school-streets, Natural Philosophy. After which, within less than three years space, I was won, by entreaty of my best affected friends, to stand for the Proctorship, to which I, and my colleague Mr. Bearblock of Exeter College, were quietly elected in the year 1569, without any competition, or countersuit of any other.

in making Hornchurch cricket famous for several years from 1820 onwards. John was Deputy Lieutenant of the County and a churchwarden. He died on January 1st, 1872, at the age of 71 years, and was the last of the family to occupy the Hall.

The Bearblock family have left their mark in various works and memorials erected in the church and churchyard, some of which are mentioned in other parts of this book.

During the occupation of the Bearblocks the great Tithe Barn belonging to the Hall was burnt down. This took place in March 1859. That barn was reputed to be the largest in all Essex, and the present barn which replaced it is also considered to be amongst the big barns of the County. It was this latter barn which was used for the Church Services during the restoration of the Church in 1870-1, and there are many villagers still living who are able to assert that they were christened in the Great Tithe Barn of Hornchurch Hall.

Mr. Brooks Gooch followed Mr. John Bearblock as lessee of the Hall, his occupation extending to Michaelmas 1884, when Mr. John B. Gill, the present lessee, entered into occupation. The land owned by New College at the present time in connection with Hornchurch Hall comprises 274 acres.

The Manor of Suttons.

The Manor of Suttons, previously mentioned as forming part of the lands granted to the Hostel of St. Bernard de Monte Jovis, is now known as Suttons Farm. The present house is entirely modern, there being nothing remaining of the old Manor house. It is in the occupation of Mr. Thomas Crawford, and at the present time comprises 384 acres. It is situated about half a mile south of Hornchurch Station.

The name is supposed by some to denote its southern situation with respect to Hornchurch Hall, and is said to be a corruption of the word south :—Southon—Sutton. It was more likely the name of an early owner of the Manor, as most of these names are personal. Thomas Sutton, the founder of Charterhouse, had estates in

Essex in the 16th century, and the name may have some connection with him or his ancestors.

Wright gives Mr. Bricket Wennell as occupier in 1814, and in *White's Essex* of 1848 Mr. Samuel Brooks Gooch is recorded as living there. He was a church-warden of the Parish Church, and at his death was succeeded by his son Brooks Gooch, who was formerly in occupation at Hornchurch Hall.

Mr. Day followed him, and remained as lessee until 1888, when Mr. Thomas Crawford came into occupation.

The Manor of Lees Gardens.

The Manor of Lees Gardens was situated in the Wingletye Lane, and the old Manor House stood in a position about midway between Duryfalls and Wych Elm. This was the fourth Manor in the immediate vicinity of the village, but no trace of the Manor House now remains. The last occupier was Mr. John Mitchell, father of Mr. Edward Mitchell, of " Gerpins," Rainham, who was lessee of the mill. He lived at Lees Gardens from 1847 to 1869, and it then came into the possession of Mr. Thomas Woodfine, who, in an attempt to rebuild it, found it in such a decayed condition that it had to be pulled down. It is interesting to know that part of it still exists in Hornchurch to-day, some of the bricks of the old Manor House being built into the house known as " Treath," on the north side of Church Hill, owned by Mr. Thomas Gardner, and occupied by Drs. Bletsoe and Sanderson.

The description of this Manor in *Ogborne's* History of Essex is as follows :—

" The Manor of Lee's Gardens was held by Marcellinus Haylys, Esq., with two messuages, 190 acres of arable, 30 acres of meadow, 100 of pasture, 12 of marsh, and 39s. rent of Queen Elizabeth in fealty, and paying 21s. 9d. yearly rent. Thomas Hone* died seised of it in 1604, it has since passed through the families of Lord St. John, Fisher, Lewis, Probyn, Dawson and Higgs, and is now (1814) in possession of Mrs. Higgs."

Most of the land of this old Manor is now comprised in the farmlands of Mr. H. Kirkman, of " Lilliputs."

* This is evidently an error, as Thomas Hone was of Garolens, now Great Gardens Farm, Squirrels Heath. His memorial (a brass plate) in Hornchurch Church is inscribed :—" Here lyeth buryed ye body of Thomas Hone of Garolens, Gent : who died ye 7 of Septemb. 1604, being of ye age of 63, having had 6 sonns and 6 daughters."

LANGTONS.

Langtons.

Langtons is the largest private residence in the village area, and, with its ornamental gardens and lake, occupies a commanding position overlooking Grey Towers Park, which, until the later years of the 19th century, formed part of the grounds attached to it. The present mansion is of Georgian architecture and comparatively modern, but a house of the same name occupied the site in the 17th century, as John Ellison is recorded as having resided there in the year 1657*. There is now, however, very little, if anything, of the original structure traceable ; the oldest building being the small bath house in the garden, the pump of which bears the date 1760, and the initials " J. M." During the latter part of the 18th century, and the first half of the 19th century, Langtons was owned and occupied by the Massu family, who were Huguenot refugees, and who had become wealthy silk merchants in the City of London. It is probable that the initials on the pump, above mentioned, may have been placed there to commemorate the birth year of John Massu, who died in 1807, aged 47. His widow, Mrs. Mary Massu, continued to reside at Langtons for many years after his decease, and died there in 1850, In that year Mr. John Wagener became possessed of it. He continued in occupation until his death in 1884 and after his decease his wife lived there until she died in 1891. The property then came into the hands of Colonel Henry Holmes, from whom it was purchased by Mr. W. Varco Williams, the present occupier, in 1899.

Mr. Williams is a Justice of the Peace for the County, Member of the Standing Joint Committee, and a Member of the Essex County Council, representing Dagenham Division. For over 30 years he has played a leading part in the political life of the Romford Division of Essex, and on the retirement of the late Colonel Holmes as Chairman of the Central Conservative Council he was unanimously elected to that office. Besides his many

* Also mentioned in 1606 in the Will of Thomas Barker of Marshfoot. On Carey's Surveying Map of 1786 Mr, Wyatt is given as the occupier of Langtons.

LANGTONS FROM THE PARK, SHOWING THE LAKE, AND ORANGERY (ON LEFT).

activities of a public character in the County, he has been a Member of the Port of London Authority since its inception, and has also filled the office of Master of the Watermen's Company.

Hornchurch Lodge.

Hornchurch Lodge, the beautiful ivy-covered old house in the middle of Church Hill, was in all probability built some time in the 16th century. Francis Rame (or Ram), father of that Anthony Rame who founded Rame's Charity* in 1621, is said to have lived here. The fact that the cottages from which the revenue of this Charity is drawn are adjacent to the Lodge, and doubtless at one time formed part of the property, would tend to show the connection of the Rames with it. Francis Rame was steward to Sir Anthony Cooke, tutor to Edward VI., who entertained Queen Elizabeth at Gidea Hall. The alabaster monument of Francis Rame is one of the most interesting in Hornchurch Church. It was formerly in the chancel, but is now on the wall at the west end of the church; it represents him and his wife kneeling at a faldstool, underneath being the figures of their twelve children, with the following inscription :—

Here lyeth the bodies of Francis Ram, Esq., and Helen his wife, wh. Francis departed March 19,1617, of the age of 80 years, and Helen departed July 11, 1613, of the age of 58, they lived together in holy matrimony 40 yeares having IX Sons and one Daughter.

> Their godly life and godly end
> Assureth us that gods their frend
> They died in Christ to rise againe
> Death is not losse to them but gaine
> Their faith was strong their hope was suer
> Their charitie doth still induer
> Here and in heaven even after death
> For love ends not wth mortall breath
> Their pilgrimage beinge passed well
> Christ calleth them now in heavē to dwell.

There does not appear to be any other existing records of the occupiers of Hornchurch Lodge until the year 1820, when it came into the possession of Mr. Thomas Mashiter, who occupied it until his death, at

* See page 108.

the age of 83 years, in 1862. Mr. Mashiter was High Steward of the Liberty of Havering and a Justice of the Peace, and it was his custom to use one of the small cottages facing the road just above the Lodge as his courthouse. Hornchurch Lodge was left by him to his nephew, Mr. Thomas Helme, for life, a condition of his will being that he, and all successive heirs of the family estates, (which until recently included what is now known as Mill Park Estate), should assume the name of Mashiter. On the death of Mr. Thomas Mashiter (*né* Helme) his son Edward resided at the Lodge until 1890. He was Justice of the Peace for the County, and Churchwarden of the Parish Church. During his residence Hornchurch Lodge was one of the meets of the Essex Union Foxhounds,* of which Mr. E. Mashiter was Honorary Secretary for a period of 15 years, afterwards becoming Master of the Hunt.†

Mrs. Fenner followed Mr. E. Mashiter as occupier of the Lodge, and it is now owned and occupied by Dr. Thomas Lambe.

Fairkytes.

Job Alibone, a Roman Catholic holding an official position in the London Post Office, is recorded as having lived at Fairkytes, Billet Lane, in the 17th century. His eldest son, Sir Richard Alibone, one of the Justices of the King's Bench, and the first of the Romish faith to hold that office for 150 years, was buried in Dagenham Church in 1688, where a handsome monument is erected to his memory by his widow, Dame Barbara Alibone, the daughter of John Blackstone. She was probably related to Richard Blackstone, as her arms are similar to those on his monument in Hornchurch Church.

Mr. Thomas Wedlake owned and resided at Fairkytes when he came to Hornchurch in 1784, and his occupancy probably extended well on into the 19th century.

* Another meet was the Bell at Upminster. The nearest meets are now at Cranham and North Ockendon.

† Mr. Edward Mashiter was Master of the Essex Union Foxhounds from 1898 to 1909, and on his resigning the Mastership, the Hunt presented him with his equestrian portrait, with three favorite hounds, in oils, painted by Miss Imogen Collier ; also a beautiful model of a fox in silver by Garrard, Haymarket

Photo]

FAIRKYTES.

[Bursall Tonge.

Perhaps the most interesting fact connected with Fairkytes is that there resided there for many years a son of Mrs. Elizabeth Fry the great Quakeress philanthropist and prison reformer. Mr. Joseph Fry was a worthy son of a great and good mother, and he and his wife were well known in the village for their charity and benevolence. Fairkytes was, during their occupancy, the centre of activity for all kinds of parochial, religious, and charitable work, and many were the entertainments provided by them for the village folk, more especially for the young people. They had a large family of eleven children, and one of their daughters, Augusta, was destined to follow, in some respects, in the footsteps of her illustrious grandmother. She acted for many years as Lady Visitor at Holloway Prison, and was Honorary Secretary to the " Elizabeth Fry Refuge," Mare Street, Hackney (a memorial to Elizabeth Fry), where she nobly maintained the great traditions of her family in carrying on the work for the reformation of women prisoners. During the Franco-Prussian War in 1870-71, she served as a delegate on the " War Victim's Fund," a fund collected, maintained and administered by the Society of Friends, with the object of alleviating the sufferings of, and the distribution of food and clothing to, the French people in the neighbourhood of Paris, Metz, and the Loire. She died at Biarritz on 9th March, 1898.

Mr. Joseph Fry lived to the age of 87 years, dying on Christmas Day, 1896.

On the north wall in Hornchurch Church a brass memorial plate has been erected in memory of the Fry family.

Mr. F. L. Bradley succeeded Mr. Joseph Fry in the occupation of Fairkytes, and resided there from 1897 to 1902, when it was purchased by Mr. James R. Robertson, the present occupier.

Mr. Robertson is a Member of the Institution of Civil Engineers, and holds the position of Sectional Engineer to the London, Tilbury and Southend Section of the Midland Railway. He has resided in Hornchurch since January, 1884, and formerly occupied " The Hollies " and " Thorpe Lodge."

Photo]

DURYFALLS.

[Bursall Tonge.

"Duryfalls."

The beautiful creeper-clad residence at the corner of Wingletye Lane is, with the exception of Nelmes and Hornchurch Hall, reputed to be the oldest house in the village. It was originally a farmhouse, and is believed to have. formed part of the Manor of Lees Gardens. The house is of somewhat remarkable construction, being built on a framework of solid baulks of oak, roughly hewn, which are left exposed throughout the whole of the interior. The origin of the name "Duryfalls" has often been the subject of conjecture. One would naturally associate such a name with something by way of a waterfall, but anyone who knows the position would be hardly likely to suggest that any such had ever been in the vicinity. I think, however, a reason for the name may be found in the fact that one, Durrifalls, is mentioned in the Parish Registers in the 16th century. Houses in those days were commonly called after the persons who owned, or lived in them, and it is therefore probable that Durrifalls lived in this house. It is mentioned again, and this time as a house, in 1633, when Peter Webb* was baptised from there. The corner of Wingletye Lane, on which stands "Duryfalls," was known as Doggett's Corner. Mr. Doggett was one of the Churchwardens in 1779, and doubtless also lived at "Duryfalls."

There appear to be no records of the early occupiers of "Duryfalls," other than those above mentioned. Mrs. Woodfine occupied it for some years prior to 1885, when it was purchased by Mr. Thomas Gardner, the present occupier.

Mr. Gardner is a Justice of the Peace for the County, and has represented Hornchurch on the Essex County Council since 1898. He was elected Chairman of the Hornchurch School Board in 1889, and continued to act as Chairman of the Hornchurch School Managers when the control of the Elementary Schools passed to the County Council. He served on the Parish Council as Chairman in the years 1897, 1898, 1899 and 1900.

* June 29, 1633 :—Peter Webb, son of Richard, born at Durifalls (Parish Registers).

SUTTONS GATE.

Suttons Gate.

This fine old house in Suttons Lane was, in the middle of the 17th century, the residence of Sir Francis Prujean, Knight, M.D., President of the College of Physicians. He married Margaret, daughter of Thomas Legatt, of Hornchurch Hall, who was the lessee of a great part of the Hornchurch property belonging to New College. Sir Francis died on June 23rd, 1666, and in his will he says :—

" My body I leave to the earth from whence it came, to be buried in Hornchurch near my late deceased wife, and have a decent monument there."

He died at his house in the Old Bailey, London, the site of which is still called Prujean Square. He was, however, buried at Hornchurch, as he desired, and a marble monument with a long Latin inscription, was erected to his memory in Hornchurch Church.

Sir Francis was succeeded by his son Thomas Prujean, M.D., and at the death of the latter, his son Robert inherited Suttons Gate under the Will of his great uncle, Thomas Legatt. This Robert Prujean, however, became a Roman Catholic and retired to a monastery in Flanders.

John Cooper was living at Suttons Gate in the early part of the 19th century. A tablet is erected in Hornchurch Church to his memory and that of his wife. He died in 1844. Near this memorial, on the south side of the west end of the church, is a stained glass window to the memory of William Henry Cooper, of Stoke D'Abernon, Surrey, who died on 25th March, 1878. He was doubtless a descendant of the John Cooper above mentioned.

In 1848 Charles Clarke was living at Suttons Gate, and was followed by Robert Lambert, who died 26th October, 1863.

Mr. Charles Osborne May became possessed of it in 1877, and since his death in 1913 his widow has continued to reside there.

This house is not called Suttons Gate without reason, for there was originally a gate across the roadway there, It was on the north or village side of the house, and just below the little lodge still standing there. The gate was removed about 80 years ago.

[Frank Luff.

GREY TOWERS.

Photo]

Grey Towers.

As a family residence " Grey Towers " has known only one occupier. It was built by Lieut. Colonel Henry Holmes, D.L., J.P., in 1876-7, and was occupied by him at Christmas 1876. It is a castellated mansion in the style of the 12th century, and is now well overgrown with ivy and other creepers. A feature of the interior is a handsome black and white marble staircase, rising out of a finely decorated hall, with a ceiling of carved oak, and a stained glass window at the head of the first flight of stairs. The house is approached by an avenue of lime trees, at the entrance gates being two castellated lodges in keeping with the architecture of the house. There are beautiful terrace gardens leading down to an ornamental lake, and the adjoining " Grey Towers " Park has been the scene of all the important local and parochial celebrations for many years past. In it was also the famous pitch of the Village Cricket Club.

Colonel Holmes came of an old and influential Durham Quaker family, and was the son of Mr. John Gilbert Holmes, a north country shipbuilder. He was himself a shipbuilder and shipowner, with shipyards at Middlesborough and offices in the city of London, where he carried on an extensive business. He was one of the first to realise the approaching end of the era of the wooden ship, and to recognise the enormous possibilities of iron and steel ship building. He was a Director of the London City and Midland Bank, and was for some years joint proprietor of the Old Hornchurch Brewery.

Before occupying Grey Towers he resided at Harwood Hall, Corbets Tey, but it was during his long residence in Hornchurch that he identified himself so largely with County and local affairs. In 1882 he raised a Battery (No. 9, Hornchurch Battery) of the First Essex Artillery Volunteers, of which Corps he afterwards became Colonel. He was Chairman of the local Bench of Magistrates, Chairman of the Central Conservative Council for the Romford Division of Essex, and was the first representative for the Parish of Horn-

GREY TOWERS CAMP UNDER SNOW.

church on the Essex County Council. He was also the first Chairman of the Hornchurch School Board. For some 30 years his house was the centre of the social and political life of the village and neighbourhood, while he himself was a leader in all the philanthropic and charitable movements in the district.

Colonel Holmes married Emilie Helena Mary, elder daughter of Mr. John Wagener, of " Langtons," and their golden wedding was celebrated on the 20th October, 1913, which happy event was very shortly afterwards followed by the Colonel's death. He died at the advanced age of 85 years on the 3rd December, 1913, esteemed and beloved as an honourable gentleman and a capable man of affairs. He left a widow, five sons, and one daughter.

Mrs. Holmes survived him by only a few months, her death occurring on the 19th April, 1914, at the age of 69 years.

A handsome marble monument marks the place of their burial in Hornchurch Churchyard.

Soon after the outbreak of the Great War " Grey Towers " became the Headquarters and Barracks of the First Sportsman's Battalion (23rd Royal Fusiliers) ; and after their departure in June, 1915, the Pioneers, or Navvies' Battalion, (26th Middlesex) were quartered there. It was then occupied by the New Zealand Contingent, first as their Base Camp in England, and afterwards as their Convalescent Hospital.*

Wych Elm.

Wych Elm (anciently spelled " Whychelme ") in Wingletye Lane, owned and occupied by Mr. Thomas W. Catherwood, is one of the oldest and most picturesque of the ancient houses of Hornchurch. It formed part of the Manor of Lees Gardens, and took its name from a magnificent wych elm tree, of abnormal proportions, which once stood in front of the house.

Mr. Richard Harding Newman lived at Wych Elm in the first half of the last century.

* It is intended to deal fully with the Military History of " Grey Towers " in the companion book to this :—" Hornchurch during the Great War."

Photo]

WYCH ELM.

[Bursall Tonge.

Capel Nelmes.

Capel Nelmes is a somewhat rambling place, having a courtyard enclosed on three sides. The oldest portion of the building is believed to have been the chapel* belonging to Nelmes Manor House, and probably dates from the same period as the early part of Nelmes. After passing through various vicissitudes, it was converted, about 50 years ago, into two small dwelling houses. At the same time the stables, coachhouses and groom's quarters were built on to it, while other old buildings in the immediate neighbourhood were removed. Further additions and alterations have been made during the last few years by the present owner and occupier, Mr. C. A. Jensen, who has succeeded in creating a commodious old-world dwelling house, in which the most interesting features are a large and lofty hall, with a wide open fireplace of oak and stone in the Elizabethan style and an old oak Elizabethan staircase, which originally stood in the oldest portion of Nelmes.

In two of the bedrooms in the oldest part of Capel Nelmes, the roofs are open, and the venerable oak rafters show between the plaster. These rooms are, in consequence, relatively lofty. In the other rooms the ceilings are very low, and some massive oak beams may be seen, which are still in fair condition.

The places where the large windows of the chapel originally existed at the east and west ends, as well as the doorway on the north side, may be still distinctly traced in the brickwork. On the north side the original small windows, high up near the eaves, have, for the most part, been utilized for lighting some of the upper rooms.

The whole of the original glass of the windows has entirely disappeared, and the present glass is mostly modern, the remainder being that which was used in the conversion of the building into cottages, as pre-

* Although there appears to be no authentic records of the existence of a Chapel at Nelmes, Dr. Thomas Harding Newman, while living at the manor house, gave it as his opinion that a chapel at one time occupied the position on which " Capel Nelmes " now stands. This information was conveyed to me by ⊕Mrs. Ward, wife of the Rev. T. W. Ward, Vicar of Rainham, Essex. Mrs. Ward is a daughter of the late Richard Harding Newman, Esq., and was cousin to Dr. Newman.

viously mentioned. The brick mullions and jambs to the windows have at one period been encased in cement, similar to the window in the east gable, as traces of this are to be found where it has been renewed.

The preservation of the remains of this ancient building has, in a special way, helped to sustain the antiquarian interest in an important part of the most celebrated manor in the neighbourhood.

Lilliputs.

Lilliputs is situated on the east side of Wingletye Lane, and is approached by a winding " chase " from Hay Green. Owing to its somewhat isolated position, it is not so well known as many of the ancient houses of Hornchurch, but it is nevertheless one of the oldest and most charming residences in the parish. There is a moat, with a picturesque old-world grass walk, on the west side of the house, and on the wall by the gateway there still remains one of the ancient mounting steps used by ladies when mounting their horses.

In the first half of the nineteenth century, Mr. Peter Esdaile Bearblock owned and occupied Lilliputs. He was a son of the Rev. James Bearblock, of Hornchurch Hall, and largely identified himself with the formation and maintenance of the 15th Essex Rifles, in which he served as Captain. During his occupancy of Lilliputs the shooting range of the Corps was in a meadow adjoining the house. He died on December 21, 1869, at the age of 69 years, and was buried in the family vault in Hornchurch Churchyard.

For many years Lilliputs was owned by Mr. Alfred Savill, and it is still in possession of his trustees. In 1886 Mr. Benjamin Kirkman became lessee of the house, and of the adjoining farmland, which, for the most part, was formerly included in the old Manor of Lees Gardens. Mr. Benjamin Kirkman was followed by his son, Ernest, as occupier, and at his death in 1913 his brother, Mr. Henry Kirkman, the present lessee, entered into occupation.

At the bend of the chase is the site of another old house, known as Drywoods, which was pulled down

LILLIPUTS.

some few years ago. This house was one of the best known houses in the olden days, and was frequently mentioned in the Parish records.

Harrow Lodge.

Harrow Lodge is situated in the Hornchurch Road, and is approached by an avenue. The present house was built in 1787. It was formerly part of the Harrow Lodge Estate, owned by Mr. Edward Bousfield Dawson, but is now in the possession of the Guardians of the parish of St. Leonard, Shoreditch. The Rev. George Clayton is given in *White's Essex* as the occupier in 1848. Mr. Henry Kirkman, who farmed the adjacent farmlands, was lessee from 1904 to 1913, and it is now in the occupation of Mr. A. Stone.

Ford Lodge.

Although not actually in the village area, Ford Lodge, situated in Ford Lane, South Hornchurch, is one of the most ancient houses in the parish. A house by that name has stood there for some centuries, but there is very little recorded history in connection with it. The present building was either built or restored by Christopher Tyler of Whybridges in about the year 1750, and the property remained in that family until nearly the end of the 19th century. In 1854 Mrs. Deborah Tyler,* who was then about 95 years of age, was living there with her three daughters, the last of whom died in 1884. The property then passed to the Mashiter family, one, Octavius Mashiter, having many years before married an elder daughter of Mrs. Tyler.

Among the later owners and occupiers of Ford Lodge were Mr. W. G. Softly and Mr. R. E. d'Ascoli.

EDWARD THE CONFESSOR

(1042—1066).

Havering-atte-Bower was the favourite retreat of several of our Saxon Kings and of many monarchs of a later period, but it came more prominently into notice as a royal residence in the reign of Edward the Con-

* *White's Essex* gives " Mrs. Deborah Tyler farmeress " as occupying Ford Lodge in 1848.

fessor. Here he often held his court, and here, it is said, he died.

The King's bower, or palace, was at that time within the confines of the parish of Hornchurch, and as a consequence Hornchurch may aspire to the title of a royal village. While it is incontrovertible that a considerable part of the Confessor's life was spent in our midst, and that therefore Hornchurch men may claim him as a brother parishioner, there is very little recorded fact to connect him with our village, and it is rather historical narrative, more or less of a legendary character, that associates him with our locality. There are few prettier stories than that which connects him with the supposed naming of Havering in the giving of a ring to a beggar man.

That incident is said to have taken place at the consecration of a church in Essex, at which Edward the Confessor was present. After the ceremony a fair old man approached the King begging alms of him, in the name of God and St. John the Evangelist. The King, having no money on him, and his almoner not being in his company, took the ring from his finger and gave it to the beggar man with the words " Have a ring ! " Some years after, some English pilgrims were travelling in the Holy Land, and, at night fall, having lost their way, saw in the distance a company clothed in white moving in procession, preceded by lights, and followed by a fair ancient man. The pilgrims coming up with the procession, the old man, who was of princely bearing, enquired who they were, and whence they came. On hearing their story he invited them to accompany him, and brought them to a beautiful city, and lodged them for the night in a splendid apartment, where they were treated with great hospitality and regaled with all kinds of eastern delicacies. On the morrow he sent them on their way, and at parting told them he was John the Evangelist, adding, so the legend goes :—

" Say ye untoe Edwarde your king, that I grete hym well by the token that he gaaf to me this ryng with hys own handes, at the hallowyng of my chirche ; which rynge ye shall deliver hym agayn, and say ye to him, that wythin six monethes he shall be in the joye of heven wyth me, where he shall have his rewarde for his chastite and for his good lyvinge."

On their return to England the pilgrims made their way to the Bower at Havering and delivered to the King their message and the ring, and it is said that he soon afterwards fell sick, distributed his wealth to the poor, and prepared for death.

He died on January 5th, 1066, and was buried in Westminster Abbey, where, in the Chapel dedicated to his memory, the whole story is told in sculpture, and is likewise painted on one of the windows. It also appears on the east window of the south aisle of St. Edward's Church, Romford. The symbol of the ring occupies a prominent place on the Elizabethan seal of the Royal Liberty of Havering.

The ring which is placed upon the finger of the Sovereigns of England at their coronation, is said to be the actual ring connected with this beautiful, if legendary story.

Hornchurch folk love to imagine that the church where the incident of the ring took place* was the building which preceded the present edifice on the hilltop, and was supposed by some to have been built by Edward the Confessor himself. However legendary the latter part of the story may be, the giving of the ring to the beggar man is generally believed to have some foundation in fact, and if that be so, it is not unreasonable to attach it to the church which for many centuries,

Drawn by A. B. Bamford

EDWARD THE CONFESSOR,
from the window in Hornchurch Church.

* Wright's *History of Essex* gives Clavering as the Church where the incident took place.

58

indeed down to the reign of Henry II., was known as Ecclesia de Havering, or the Church of Havering.*

The figure of the Confessor is depicted in the old grisaille window at the eastern end of the north chancel of St. Andrew's Church.

THE OLD MONASTERY OR PRIORY OF HORNCHURCH.

With the exception of the association of Edward the Confessor with Hornchurch, nothing stands out so prominently in the ancient history of the place as the episode which connects it with the Monks of St. Bernard of Savoy, the story of whose ministrations in the everlasting snows of the Alps is well known. St. Bernard of Savoy is not to be confused with St. Bernard, first Abbot of Clairvaux, one of the "fathers" of the church, who was born in 1071 and died in 1153. St. Bernard of Savoy is surnamed de Menthone, and was son of Richard Baron de Menthone. Born in Savoy in the year 923, he died at Novare au Milanois on May 28, 1008. His "day" in the calendar is June 15. In spite of the opposition of his parents, he devoted himself to an ecclesiastical life, and after studying at Paris, he is said to have retired to Aouste (Aosta) in Piemont, where he received holy orders. He employed himself in preaching and especially in missions in the mountains of the Alps. He built a monastery and a "hospital" on the high mountain of Valois, near to a spot where there had been, it is said, a temple to Jupiter. This temple he is stated to have demolished. It is on this account that the hospital is called "the hospice of St. Bernard de Monte Jovis" (St. Bernard of the mountain of Jupiter).

In the winter of 1158-1159 envoys of the King of England, while crossing the Alps by the Great St. Bernard Pass, were succoured and liberally entertained by the Brotherhood of the Hospital of St. Bernard,

* Morant derives the name of Havering from the Saxon " haefer," a goat, and " ing "a meadow, but Terry says it is quite as likely derived from " Havre," the Danish word for " o its " This probability is strengthened by the fact of the Danish connection with this locality ; Havering would accordingly signify " Oat meadow."

E

and on the return of the envoys to this country, Henry II., hearing of the hospitality accorded to his representatives, presented to "the Hospice of St. Bernard de Monte Jovis in the Diocese of Sedum or Syon in Savoy" property for the endowment of a religious house and church at Havering in Essex. And so it came about that the Cell, or Hospice, of St. Nicholas and St. Bernard was established in Hornchurch. Henry II. endowed it with the manors of Hornchurch Hall and Suttons (with some advantages in Havering), and in the year 1160 a Prior and twelve Monks of St. Bernard commenced their ministrations in our village.

In addition to these two manors, the monastic establishment possessed a house in Fenchurch Street, known as Prior's Inn, which was occupied by the Prior on his visits to London. Stow, in his *Survey of London* (1633), thus refers to this house :—

"Then have ye on the South side of Fenne-church Street, over against the wall or pumpe, amongst other faire and well builded houses, one that sometime belonged to the Prior of Monte Jovis, or Monasteria Cornuta—a cell to Monte Jovis beyond the seas—in Essex. It was the prior's inne, when he repaired to this Citie."

A little more than a century later, in 1263, Peter, Earl of Savoy and Richmond, bestowed on the Monastery the house built by him in the Strand, called *The Savoy*, but this house was in 1270 purchased for £200, from the Monastery, by Peter's niece, Eleanor, Queen of Henry III., for her son Edmund, Earl of Lancaster.

Unfortunately all trace of the Monastery at Hornchurch has now disappeared, but there has been considerable speculation as to where it stood. One authority is of opinion that it was on the spot where the old White Hart Inn stood. That ancient hostelry, which was burnt down in 1872,* was known to contain some architectural remains of an ecclesiastical character belonging to the Early English or Pointed period, which might have had some connection with the Cell. Many think that it was on a spot where North Street strikes off at right angles to High Street.

* See page 22.

J. A. Repton, the eminent landscape gardener, of Hare Street, believed the site to have been in the Millfield, and his reason for this is given in Ogborne's *History of Essex*, as follows :—

"All that remains is an artificial mound near the Windmill in the field by the Churchyard. This seems to have been a broad esplanade of about 300 paces long, and raised about 6 or 7 feet above the natural level. It appears to have been a walk, probably in the south front of the Monastery, and is remarkable for the east end pointing to Upminster spire, at the distance of one mile, and to the west by Limehouse church."

For a period of about 230 years successive Priors and Monks from the great Hospice of St. Bernard continued their ministrations in Hornchurch, and then negotiations took place which resulted in the ecclesiastical jurisdiction of the Parish passing to New College, Oxford. About the year 1392, William of Wykeham obtained from the Pope and from Richard II. permission to purchase from the Hospital of St. Bernard de Monte Jovis all the lands and revenues belonging to the subordinate establishment at Hornchurch, in order to endow his New College at Oxford, the building of which took eight years, having been commenced on March 5, 1379, and completed on April 14, 1387. And so, for a period of over 500 years, the Warden and Fellows of New College have received the revenues of the lands and Manors of Hornchurch Hall and Suttons, and, in return, have ministered to the spiritual needs of the parish through their Chaplains, or Vicars Temporal, 37 of whom—including the present Chaplain, Rev. Herbert Dale, M.A.—have officiated in that capacity.

HOW HORNCHURCH GOT ITS NAME.

Many are the conjectures as to how our village came by its name. Most of the recognised authorities on Essex history have advanced at least one theory on the subject. In the present chapter I have set out most of the opinions which have obtained some acceptance by those who, over a long period of time, have given their attention to the elucidation of an interesting problem which has never yet been satisfactorily solved.

I have already given one view, on page 4, viz. :—
that of the *Rev. W. Pallin,* who, in his " Stifford and
its Neighbourhood," connects the currying industry
and its trade emblem of " a pair of horns " with the
Church—hence Hornchurch.

Morant inclined to the opinion that the epithet
Cornuta (horned) was derived from the crest belonging
to the mother Monastery in Savoy, to which that of
Hornchurch was a subordinate, the great Hospital of
St. Bernard de Monte Jovis in Savoy having been,
according to tradition, as already stated, built upon the
site of a pagan temple which was dedicated to Jupiter—
hence called Mons Jovis—and that the horns were
preserved in memory of Jupiter, being sometimes represented with horns. Against this theory it must be
stated that there is no evidence that the monastery
referred to ever used a horn or horns in any armorial
bearings. On the contrary the arms used by the Order
contained no such emblem. Morant cites no authority
and it must be assumed that his statement was con-
jectural.

Salmon believed it to be only a contraction of Have-
ring-Church.

John Audrey, the antiquarian, was of opinion that :
" Hornchurch in Essex hath its denomination from the
horns of a hart that happened to be killed by the King's
dog, near the church, as it was building, and the horns
were put in the walls of the Church."

Another explanation of the name which finds favour
with many modern archæologists has the merit of
simplicity and also of analogy with the origin of other
place names. This derivation is that Hornchurch
means the church of Horn—Horn being a personal
name. Thus Hornby (Lincolnshire) is supposed to
be the dwelling of Horn. Hornsea (East Riding)—in
Domesday *Hornesse*—is " the isle of Horn " ; Horn-
castle, " the camp of Horn " ; Horningsham (Wilt-
shire) " the home of the sons of Horn." (As to these
and other kindred derivations see Johnston's *Place
Names* 1915.) It is noteworthy that East Horndon
and West Horndon are both within about eight miles
of Romford ; and that Horndon-on-the-Hill is about

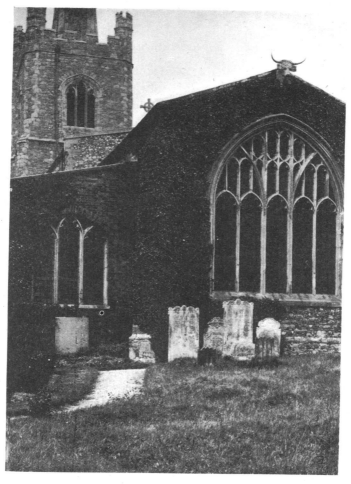

ST. ANDREW'S CHURCH, EAST END.

ten miles from Romford. It may be doubted, however, whether East and West Horndon can be regarded as analogous with Hornchurch since they were formerly known as Thorndon and in Domesday appear as Torindone, Torninduna, Thornyndon and Westtorendon. But Horndon-on-the-Hill, which is Horninduna in Domesday, is presumably derived from the personal name Horn, the name of some former lord or chieftain. " Horn," the hero of the well-known Old English metrical romance, dating from the 13th century, is represented as son of Murray (otherwise Allof), King of " Sudenne," which some have supposed to mean Surrey and Sussex. Horn's father was slain by Saracen pirates, and Horn himself was turned adrift with twelve other children of the King. After various adventures he married Rymenhild, daughter of the King of Westenesse (Cornwall ?), and reconquered his father's kingdom. The legend states that when disguised as a palmer Horn made himself known to his bride, Rymenhild, by dropping a ring into the cup which she offered him. This King Horn does not seem to have been traditionally associated in any way with Essex or the East of England. Assuming that Hornchurch may have been a church named in honour of some personage named Horn,the subsequent introduction of the horns in the church fabric might be considered as only a punning allusion to the name. The Latinised forms " Ecclesia Cornuta " and " Monasterium Cornutum " would also be in accordance with mediæval custom.

THE PARISH CHURCH.

The history of a place centres largely round its Parish Church, and especially is this so when the church is a grand and venerable pile like that of St. Andrew's on the top of the hill : hoary with age and weatherbeaten with the storms, elemental and temporal, of many centuries. There would appear to be little doubt that for about a thousand years a church has stood on, or near, the site of the present edifice, though there is nothing traceable in this building earlier than the fourteenth century.

64

Ford's Real Photo, Ilford.　　INTERIOR OF ST. ANDREW'S CHURCH, HORNCHURCH.

In the time of Edward the Confessor (1042-1066) it was the only church in what in later years came to be known as the Royal Liberty of Havering, with the exception of a small chapel near the Palace of the King at Havering-atte-Bower, used exclusively by the royal household. Mr. A. R. Hope Moncrieff, in his interesting book "*Essex*," so beautifully illustrated by Mr. L. Burleigh Bruhl, speaks of the church of Hornchurch as "*the Westminster of the Royal precincts.*" He again refers to it as "*the celebrated church,*" in the following

Photo]   THE CHAPLAINCY.   [*Bursall Tonge.*

reference to Hornchurch : "The village itself is still a museum of plastered, gabled and overhanging fronts. . . . . . At the south end one turns east for the celebrated church, its spire rising above a broken bosky hollow, known as the Millfield."

St. Andrew's is in the rural deanery of Chafford (otherwise Romford), the archdeaconry of Essex and the diocese of Chelmsford, of which the first and present

Bishop is the Right Rev. John E. Watts-Ditchfield, D.D. There are, perhaps, few parish churches in England where there are so many ecclesiastical peculiarities as are connected with our own church. In the first place it is the only church in the Kingdom which has a bull's head and horns at the east end, instead of a cross. Its incumbent is, in reality, neither simply a Vicar nor a Rector, but a Chaplain and Vicar Temporal,* being so described in the Deed of his presentation to the living. He lives in a beautiful old house opposite the church, over the front door of which are the Arms of New College, Oxford, with its motto—immortalized by William of Wykeham—" Manners makyth man," and this residence is not a Vicarage, neither is it a Rectory, but it is a private house belonging to New College, and is called "The Chaplaincy."

Then again, the churchyard provided for centuries the only burial place in the whole of the Havering district, and even Romford, long after it had become quite a considerable town, and probably much larger than Hornchurch as far as population was concerned, was obliged to bring its dead for interment in Hornchurch Churchyard. It was not until the year 1410 that the parishioners of Romford petitioned for and obtained a burial place of their own, and Havering had no similar accommodation until 1718. Even at the present day Hornchurch Churchyard is still the burial place for Harold Wood, Ardleigh Green, North West Hornchurch, South Hornchurch and the village.

†The Church, which has seating accommodation for 500, consists of a nave, with north and south aisles, chancel with north and south aisles, tower and porch.

The nave and north and south aisles are separated by arcades of four arches with three columns and two responds on either side and are of the Decorated period of Edward I. or II., which would seem to indicate the period when this church was built ; the details of the capitals, which are all alike, are very

* When referring to the Incumbent of Hornchurch in these pages I have, for the sake of convenience and in accordance with the general custom of the place, styled him Vicar.

† The technical details concerning the architecture of the Church have been mainly compiled from an article by Mr. Fred Chancellor, F.R.I.B.A., which appeared in *The Essex Review* for January, 1896, No. 17, vol. v.

good. On the north side, in the spandril between the two western arches, is a quatrefoil sunk in the stonework, with a flower carved in each eye of the quatrefoil and in the centre. There has been some speculation as to the meaning of this quatrefoil, but it is generally supposed that it was introduced for decorative purposes only, and that it was originally intended to place similar ornaments between the other arches. These two arcades are all that now remain of the early church, except, perhaps, the sedilia in the chancel, to be alluded to hereafter.

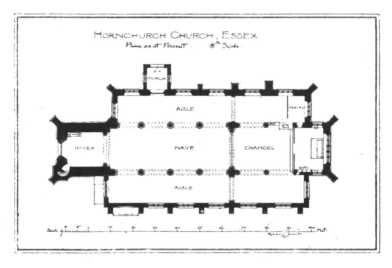

Nearly 100 years after the erection of these arcades, the present clerestory was added ; it consists of four 3-light Perpendicular windows on either side. Those on the north side are, except where they have been repaired in cement, in their original condition, but the clerestory on the south side has been rebuilt in modern times in red and stock bricks, with the old stonework of windows, deprived of the external jambs and arches, and with their internal stone quoins built into the modern work ; they are throughout of the same design.

The chancel is separated from the nave by a chancel arch ; the clustered shaft on the north side is original, but that on the south side is modern, as are also the caps and bases of both and the chancel arch itself. It is noticeable that the chancel arch is not in the centre of the nave, and, apparently, in restoring this arch, the centre line of the arch was arranged to be equidistant between the clerestory walls, and not equidistant between the arcades, which would bring the arch out of centre of the nave owing to the set-back formed in the wall immediately over the arcade when the south clerestory wall was rebuilt.

The chancel has an arcade on either side of one octagonal column, and two responds with two arches. The arcades are of the Perpendicular period ; the shafts are octagonal and the splays of the arches are very much curved. Over these arches was originally a 3-light clerestory window on both sides : that on the south side has been wholly, and that on the north side, partially built up.

On the south side of the chancel is a triple sedilia constructed with four shafts supporting cusped heads of Decorated character, and of the same date as the nave arcades. The western one is pierced with a hagioscope.

There is also a piscina to the east of the sedilia, but all the stonework appears to be modern, and therefore it may be a restoration, or otherwise, of the original one.

On the north side is a modern credence, and a priest's door, very narrow and with a very pointed arch.

The chancel is lighted with two 2-light Perpendicular windows, one on either side, where it projects beyond the chancel aisles, and also by a 5-light Perpendicular east window of coloured glass.

There are seven windows in the north aisle and north chancel, and seven in the south aisle and south chancel ; five of which contain coloured glass of modern date. In the east window of the north chancel there are some fragments of old glass. In the centre light is our Saviour on the Cross, but the head appears to be that of the Virgin, which apparently got worked in by mistake when the window was restored. Over the head is a label with the letters I.N.R., the final I being missing. This window also contains the picture of Edward the Confessor, and fragments of several coats of arms. It is known as the Edward the Confessor window.

The reredos is of stone, as are also the pulpit and font, all being modern.

As far as can be ascertained the woodwork of the roof belongs to a modern restoration, with the exception of one or two beams in the chancel roof.

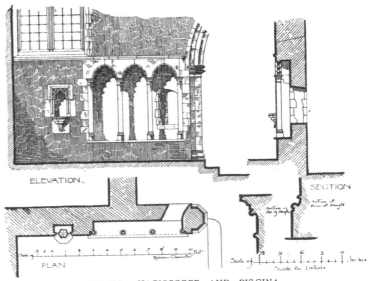

ELEVATION.

SECTION

PLAN

SEDILIA, HAGIOSCOPE AND PISCINA

The north porch has a pointed arched opening in front, and on either side is a modern 2-light Perpendicular window. The door is the original oak door, and is somewhat richly pannelled, with cusped tracery and other good detail.

The tower is a fine specimen of Perpendicular work, with a noble arch connecting it with the nave. The arch of the west doorway is pointed, enclosed in a square head very similar in design to the north doorway, but all the stonework has been incased with cement. The door itself is original, but not so rich in design as the north door, and is not in such good preservation.

Photo, Fred Gandon.]   [*By permission of Luffs, Hornchurch.*
NORTH PORCH.

Over the doorway is a 3-light Perpendicular window, modern and executed in Portland stone. In the ringing chamber (which is open to the nave) are three single-light windows, and the belfry is lighted by four 3-light windows. The tower is finished with a bold embattled parapet, with a hexagonal turret at each angle, the one containing the steps being somewhat larger than the others. Massive beams form the foundation of the spire, which is braced and strengthened in every direction and is well worthy of a visit, as it is really a fine specimen of carpentry, and has stoutly withstood the many gales to which, in its exposed position, it must have been subject during the long period of its existence. The spire, which was formerly sheathed in lead or shingles, is now covered with copper. From the base of the spire and parapet of the tower is obtained a fine panoramic view of the surrounding country.

The general construction of the tower and church is of ragstone and other stone and flints. The tower walls on the ground story are 4ft. 6in. thick, decreasing to about 3ft. in the belfry.

On the west face of the parapet of the staircase is carved what appears to be a bishop seated with upraised hands, which is generally supposed to represent William of Wykeham. There is also on the west face of the tower, over the string under the single-light window of the ringing chamber, a stone with the letter W reversed cut upon it. This is assumed to be the monogram of William of Wykeham, who, somewhere about the years 1392—1398, built the tower and in all probability rebuilt or restored the whole fabric ; but why the W is reversed and made to look more like the letter M it is difficult to understand ; perhaps it was carelessness on the part of the mason, or possibly the bishop's own way of writing his monogram of the two-fold W.

On the battlement of the tower may also be seen Rff or RII. More than one reason has been assigned for this, the most probable being that they stand for Richard II., in whose reign the tower was built.

The tower and spire* rise to a height of 120 feet. That the spire was not built at the same time as the tower is somewhat common knowledge, but if it needed proof it could be found in the will of Thomas Scargill,

* The spire was built about 70 years later than the tower.

who died at Bretons in 1476, and who made the following bequest to the church :—

Item :—I will to the making of the steple att Hornechurche X marcs* when they shall begin the saide steple.

This same benefactor also made two other rather curious bequests to the church, which are set out in the following quaint manner :—

" In the name of God, Amen. The xvii. day of the month of August 1475—15 of King Edward 4. I Thomas Scargill, squyer, being in gode memory & hole mynde, thanked be God. My soule to Almighty God, my maker and Sauiour, & to His blessed moder Mary the Virgin, & to all the holy company of heuen. . . . ."

Item :—I wyll & bequethe to the high awter of Hornechurche vjs. : viiid.†

Item :—I will that there be gouen & delivred the day of my burieing among powr peple to pray for my sowle xls.‡

Item :—I will that Master William Vicar of Hornechurche have a chaleys for to pray for my soule & all my frendes.

The chancel walls are built of rubble stone, flint and septaria, with some fragments of Roman brick. There are two good angle buttresses to the chancel.

The walls of the south aisles have been rebuilt in brick.

It is believed that when this church was rebuilt, at the end of the fourteenth or beginning of the fifteenth century, there were embattled parapets to the nave, chancel, north and south aisles and porch. They probably became dilapidated, and when the roofs were releaded at the end of the eighteenth or beginning of the nineteenth century, it was found that the easiest and cheapest mode of repair was to remove the parapets altogether, and continue the lead over the walls into a modern gutter. If these parapets were restored they would add very much to the dignity and importance of the whole building.

⁎ The lower portion of one of the buttresses on the north side appears to be original, being constructed

* Money Values :—A Mark was worth 13s. 4d. Its purchasing power in William of Wykeham's day would be at least ten times, and quite possibly twenty times. that of to-day.

† VJS : VIIId would stand for six shillings and eight pence.

‡ XLS for forty Shillings. Mr. Terry, in speaking of the high value of money in 1537. gives the following information :—" Wheat was sold @ 8s. a Quarter ; Oats @ 2s. A load of Hay was worth about 5s. A common labourer received about 16s 6d. a year, and a woman servant, who would now ask £15 to £16 a year, received 10s. a year."

similarly to the walls of the chancel ; the upper part is rebuilt in brick.

On the south side of the west door are the remains of a Stoup.

The memorials and fragments of memorials still left prove that at one time the church must have been rich in brasses and other sepulchral monuments, several of which have been mentioned in other pages of this book. One of the most important of the existing

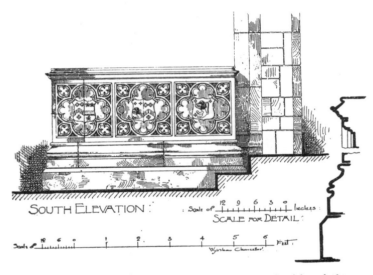

SOUTH ELEVATION :   : Scale of ⌐12 9 6 3 0 Inches :
SCALE FOR DETAIL :

Scale ⌐12 6 0   1   2.   3   4   5   6   Feet :
Wykeham Chancellor :

memorials is the Ayloffe tomb on the north side of the chancel, the description of which is as under :—

The north and south sides are divided into three panels, each panel containing a cusped quatrefoil inclosing a shield ; the west end has one similar panel with shield. Three of the shields are [sable] a lion rampant [or] collared [gules] between three crosses formy of the second. Ayloffe. Two other Shields. Ayloffe impaling [argent] a chevron between three lozenges ermine. Shawe or Shaa. One other shield Shaa impaling . . . a fess engrailed . . . between three cinquefoils . . . and the other Shield [argent] on a cross [sable] a leopard's head [or] in dexter chief a crescent for difference. Bruges or Bridges im-

74

paling Ayloffe. The brass legend from the top slab is gone, but Symonds in his notes at Herald's College gives it as follows :

Taken from ye very brass.

Off yō charite pỹ for the soule of Wīllm Ayloffe gentylman owner of the manō of Bretensse yn the County of Essex within the Lordshippe of Havering of the Bower. And also owner of grete Braksted wᵗʰ diversse other to him belonging. Which Willm. weddyed Audrey daught to Sʳ John Shawe Knight & Alderman of London et had 3 Children by the said Audrey. Wil;ᵐ Thomas et Agnes which decessid the Xᵗʰ day of August yᵉ year of Ō Lord God MVᵉXVII the IXᵗʰ yeare of the Raign of King Henry VIII. And lyeth buryed under this stone. On whose soule and all christen soules Thee have mercy. And for yō charite say a Pater Noster & Ave.

The alabaster mural monument on the north side of the tower to the memory of Thomas Witherings of Nelmes, Chief Postmaster of England in the time of Charles I., is of considerable interest, as are also the memorials to Richard Blakstone, Thomas Clutterbuck, Richard Spencer (by Flaxman) and the Fry family.

In the floor of the tower is a flat coffin-shaped stone, with a raised cross thereon on a long shaft, resting upon a stepped base, which is believed to be a memorial to one of the early Priors.

There are also four war memorials on the south wall, one in brass to the memory of Frederick John William Chester, private in H Company 1st V.B. Essex Regiment, who volunteered for active service in the South African War, and died in Pretoria, 4 July, 1900, aged 22.

The other three are 'Great War' memorials, one being in bronze to the memory of Q.M. Sergeant Charles Henry Baker, 4th Essex Regiment, who died 24 August, 1915, from wounds received in Gallipoli, 19 August, 1915, aged 31. The two others are in brass— (1) to Charles Henry Bearblock, Lieut. 9th Batt. Essex Regiment, wounded in action near Hulluch, October 20, 1915, and died the same day, aged 22 ; (2) to Walter James Bearblock, M.R.C.S., L.R.C.P., Fleet Surgeon, Royal Navy, killed in action, 31 May, 1916, when H.M.S. " Invincible " was sunk in the victory off the coast of Jutland, aged 55.

The Bells.

Hanging in the tower is one of the finest peals of bells in the county. The peal originally consisted of five bells. The exact age of these is unknown, but we have it on the authority of Messrs. Mears and Stainbank that five bells were hanging in the tower in 1552. In the year 1779 they were recast into six bells, and in 1901 two other bells were added.

The inscriptions on the bells and their sizes and weights are as follows :—

1. *Treble.* E flat. 30 inches, 5 cwts. 1 q. 4 lbs.
   "To the Glory of God & in commemoration of the 20th century. Mears me fecit A.D. 1901."

2. D. 31 inches, 5 cwts. 2 q. 16 lbs.
   "To the Glory of God & in commemoration of the 20th century. Mears me fecit A.D. 1901."

3. C 31½ inches, 5 cwts. 3 q. 20 lbs.
   "If you have a judicious ear,
   You'l own my voice is sweet & clear.
                 Mears & Co., London, fecit, 1779."

4. B flat. 34½ inches, 6 cwts. 3 q. 3 lbs.
   "Peace & good neighbourhood.
   Mears & Co., London, fecit, 1779."

5. A flat. 37⅝ inches, 8 cwts. 2 q. 18 lbs.
   "Ye ringers all that prize your health and happiness
   Be sober, merry, wise, & you'l the same possess."
                 Mears & Co., London, fecit, 1779.

6. G. 40½ inches, 10 cwts. 0 q. 13 lbs.
   "Ye people all that hear me ring,
   Be faithful to your God & King."
                 Mears & Co., London, fecit, 1779

7. F. 43⅝ inches, 14 cwts. 1 q. 25 lbs.
   "In wedlock bands all ye who join with hands and hearts unite,
   So shall our tunefull tongues combine to laud the nuptials rite."
                 Mears & Co., London, fecit, 1779.

8. Tenor. E flat. 49 inches, 18 cwts.
   The Rev. Robt. Speed, Rector, Messrs. Wennell & Doggett, Church Wardens.
   *Intactum siloe ; Percute, dulce cano :
                 1779 Wm. Mears & Co., London, fecit

The total weight of the full peal of eight bells is 3 tons 14 cwts. 3 qrs. 15 lbs.

Many famous peals have been rung on the Horn-

* Translation :—Untouched, I am silent ; Strike me, I give forth a sweet sound.

76

church bells, several of which find permanent record in the ringing chamber. The longest peal was rung on May 27, 1912, by the London Diocesan Guild and the Middlesex County Association, viz. :—a peal of Bristol Surprise Major—15,264 changes—9 hours 49 minutes. William Pye was the conductor. This peal is stated to have been " the longest length ever rung in any surprise method."

The present band of Hornchurch ringers consists of Messrs. William J. Brockhurst (Captain), John Dale, William H. Dear, Daniel Phillips, Charles Barlow, Arthur Fry, Albert Fry, John Ellis, George Adams and J. W. Brockhurst.

Mr. Isaac Dear, who has recently retired from the band, was a ringer for 58 years, and acted as Captain for many years.

The Two Pitchers in Hornchurch Church.

These Pitchers were originally made for the use of the bell ringers, and on certain occasions were filled with ale brewed at Hornchurch Hall for the refreshment of the ringers. In " The Church Bells of Essex " (Rev. Cecil Deedes and H. B. Walters, M.A., F.S.A.), it is mentioned that in the Ringing Chamber of Hornchurch belfry " there was formerly a set of old ringing rules (now superseded by a more prosaic set)," as follows :—

> If you ring with Spur or Hat*
> Three.pints of beer you pay For that ;
> If you swear or give the Lye,
> A pot you pay Immedeatly ;
> If a bell you overthrow,
> A pint you pay before you go.

T. † S. 1798.

In later years the Pitchers were used for supplying refreshment to the tenants when they came to pay their tithes at the Hall. It is evident from the inscriptions on the Pitchers that they were intended to belong to the church, but for some inexplicable reason they were in more recent times kept at the King's Head Inn

* This probably meant a man who was of better social position than a ordinary ringer, *i.e.*, one wearing hat and spurs.
A small representation of a bell is here displayed in relief.

They were seized there by Messrs. Henry and Benjamin Holmes, during the time they owned the Hornchurch Brewery, in distraint for rent, and afterwards placed in the hall at "Grey Towers." After the death of Colonel and Mrs. Holmes an auction sale was held at the "Towers," and the family "bought in" the Pitchers and presented them to the Vicar and Churchwardens, with the request that they should, if possible, always be preserved in the church.

Photo]   THE BELL RINGERS' BEER PITCHERS.   *Bursall Tonge.*

The smaller of the two is made of brownish coloured earthenware of a dull glaze, and has the following inscription in a cursive hand :—

1731.

Hornchurch, Essex.

Ringers.

John Bader	Benjn. Malin	W. Randall	} Church-wardens
Thomas White	William Carter		
Thos. Wooton	Thomas Sanger	Fra^n. Sumpner	

This pitcher is 13½ inches high and 40 inches in girth at the widest part.

The larger Pitcher is made of very dark burnt umber-coloured earthenware, and is very thickly and highly glazed, so as to become almost purple in hue. It bears the following inscription :—

MAY 24th, 1815.

This Pitcher was made by Rt. Aungier.

— Oxley	Jˢ. Fry
W. —rison	Jˢ. Nokes
John Oxley	Frⁿᵉ. Oxley
Jerg. Evrett	Samˡ. Cooper
George Hills	Peter Smith

Hornchurch Ringers, 1815.

Gift of Mr. C. Cove.

Churchwardens :—John Thompson, James Bearblock.

TOM ✝ , Lincon

The larger pitcher is 20½ inches high and 50 inches in girth at the widest part.

It is known that this pitcher was made at Mr. C. Cove's Pottery at the western end of High Street, described on page 9, and I think there is little doubt that the 1731-pitcher was also made at the same pottery, which is believed to have been established there quite 200 years ago. These pitchers should therefore be reckoned among the most cherished relics of our old village.

The Church Clock.

The present church clock, dated 1814, was made by John Thwaites and Co., Clerkenwell. It is also inscribed :—" This clock was thoroughly repaired and restored by Gillett and Johnston, Croydon, 1907."

That the church has possessed a clock for some centuries is proved by the following agreement, which appears in the parish accounts for 1674 :—

" 7th Day of December 1674 :—It was then agreed upon & bargained by & between Mr. Andrew Prime, Clock maker of Cree church Parish, London, & Mr. John Hellam of the Parish of Hornchurch, Church Warden of the same Parish, that the said Mr. Andrew Prime shall set up a new sufficient Clocke in the Church of the said Parish, with a large Dyall in the place of the old one now there standing, by the 25 Day of March next ensuing,

✝ A small representation of a bell is here displayed in relief.

And that he shall have the old Clocke & dyall, and also twenty five pounds of good and lawfull money of England of the said Church Warden or Church Wardens for the same, to be due & paid at the same day. In witnesse whereof they have both hereunto put their hands the day first above written. The Dyall to be 3 ffoot over."

The clock face was originally diamond in shape, as will be seen from the old engraving* on page 81, and it is believed that this was the clock referred to in this agreement. When, however, the present clock was installed in 1814, the diamond shaped face still remained, and " J. B.† 1814," was painted upon it. It was removed about 1850 and replaced by the present clock face.

The inscription on the Sanctus, or clock bell, which is hung outside the western side of the Tower, is :—

Donum Thomae Brandon‡
Ecclesiae Cornutae in Com : Essex.
Maii XXIX., MDCLXXIIII.

The diameter of the bell is 18½ inches, weight 1¼ cwts. (Translation of the inscription :—The gift of Thomas Brandon to the Horned Church in the County of Essex, May 29th, 1674.)

The Bellfounders' mark on the bell is a circle enclosing 3 bells.

The following entry in the parish accounts is of interest in this connection :—

" 1 Day of April 1678 :—Item :—To John Langley for lookeing to the Clocke 2 qts. of a yeare due March 25 last past 5s. 8d. ; & for the surplice washing at Christmas last & this Easter 2s. 9d. ; & for washing ye Communion Table Cloth 6d. ; & for Oyle for ye bells & clocke 6d.

The Old Chest in Hornchurch Church.

The following particulars regarding the old church chest appear in " The Church Chests of Essex " (H. William Lewer and J. Charles Wall, 1913).

" An Inventory made October 4, 6 Edward VI :—' It'm ij olde chests in the churche.'—P.R.O.K.R. *Church Goods* 2/31."

* The Rev. W. H Reynell, to whom the old engraving was inscribed, was Vicar 1786-1810.
+ These initials are assumed to be those of the Rev. James Bearblock, of Hornchurch Hall (see page 34), who was probably the donor of the Clock of 1814.
‡ Under date of Novr. 19th, 1632, there appears the following entry in the Parish Register :—" Thomas, sonne of Thomas Brandon." This was probably the record of the Baptism of the donor of the Bell.

Drawn by T. B. Clutton.   *[Engraved by J. Jeakes.*

To the Revd. William Henry Reynell, A.M. Vicar, and the Inhabitants of the Parish of Hornchurch, This North View of the Church is respectfully inscribed by their very obedient Servt. Thomas B. Clutton.

From an old Engraving in possession of the Rev. Herbert Dale, M.A.

At the Visitation made in 1668 the outgoing Churchwardens were reprimanded for retayning the keys of the chest.—*The Chests and other things Act Book, Chelmsford.*

The present Church Chest is an 18th century box bound with broad iron bands, which are fastened in position by numerous large, round & flat headed nails. The lid projects considerably over the walls of the Chest, & this is balanced by a moulded plinth. Here, however, is a curiously useless application of the iron, typical of that age when art was either debased or altogether lacking. The mediæval motif of each feature was purposeful and beautified, principles that were lost at a later period. In this instance the perpendicular iron bands on the front pass behind & below the plinth, reappearing on the front of the base, embracing the plinth, instead of binding the Chest.''

The length is 3ft. 10 in. ; width 1ft. 9 in. ; depth 1ft. 6 in.

There is an early example of an iron safe also in the vestry.

Church Restoration.

Many important works of restoration in connection with the church have been carried out in comparatively recent years.

The chancel was restored by New College in 1869, and at that time the present east window was put in to the memory of Thomas Mashiter, Esq. For many years prior to this the east window was boarded up, the Lord's Prayer, the Ten Commandments, and the Creed being painted on the boarding.

The church underwent a general restoration in 1871, during the incumbency of the Rev. Thomas Henry Griffith, at a cost of £2,000. At that time the existing oak pews were installed. They were presented by Mr. John Bearblock, of Hornchurch Hall, and his brother, Mr. Peter Esdaile Bearblock, of " Lilliputs," and did not form part of the £2,000 expended. A fine old carved oak pulpit, with overhead sounding board, was removed at the same time, and replaced by the present stone one. The work connected with the pews was carried out by Mr. James Dockrill, father of Messrs. George and Robert Dockrill.

While this work was proceeding, it was not possible to use the church for divine service, and a faculty was therefore issued by the Bishop of Rochester to the Rev T. H. Griffith, dated May 17th, 1871, authorising the use of the tithe barn at Hornchurch Hall, then leased to Mr. John Bearblock, for the church services for the time being.

The church was again restored in 1896-7, during the incumbency of the Rev. Robert Johnson, when the sum of £950 was expended. This work was carried out in accordance with plans prepared by, and under the supervision of, Mr. Fred Chancellor, F.R.I.B.A.

During the incumbency of the present Vicar, the Rev. Herbert Dale, several important works have been undertaken, the principal being :—the rehanging of the bells in 1909 ; the repairing of the top of the spire in 1910 ; the building of a new vestry and new organ in 1913 ; the installing of a new heating apparatus in 1914, and of a bell chiming apparatus in 1917. These various improvements cost upwards of £1,200.

The organ is by Henry Speechley and Sons, of Dalston. It has 3 manuals, a radiating pedal board, 22 stops, 8 couplers, 6 pneumatic pedals and 1,166 pipes.

Chaplain and Vicar Temporal.—Rev. Herbert Dale, M.A., New College, Oxford. Sometime Rural Dean of Chafford.

Assistant Curate.—Rev. A. J. Parry, A.K.C. (now Chaplain to H.M. Forces).

Churchwardens.—Mr. Walter Dendy and Mr. C. H. Baker.

Deputy do.—Mr. R. Dockrill and Mr. W. E. Langridge.

Sidesmen.—Messrs. E. Allen, A W Boulton, E G. Bratchell, W H. Brooks, T. Burden, W. Card, C. Beharell, J. Dockrill, R. Dockrill, E. Fry, G. Fry, T. Gardner, W. Halestrap, T. Johnson, W. E. Langridge, C. T. Perfect, A. J. Powell, G. Ruston, H. L. Symonds and T. W. Wedlake.

Parish Clerk and Sexton.—Arthur Cooke, Esqre., New College, M.A., M.B. ; Ch B. Oxon ; M.A. Cantab , F.R.C.S., &c.

Deputy do. do.—Mr. John Purrett.

Organist.—Mr. H. W. Alden.

LIST OF THE VICARS OF HORNCHURCH.

Name.		Date of Appointment.	Name.		Date of Appointment.
John Fowler	..	1417	Thomas Man	..	1632
William Wayfer	..	1422	William Whitaker	..	1648
John Rosson	..	1423	John Johnson	..	1655
William Sayer	..	1430	Matthew Lacock	..	1656
Jeffrey Kenchurch	..	1434	Michael Wells	..	1658
William Lowe	..	1475	Francis Shaw ..	..	1686
Thomas Skipwith	..	1478	Thomas Roberts	..	1696
William Hokyll	..	1487	Henry Levitt	..	1721
George Reede	..	1494	Francis Pyle	..	1725
Thomas Duke	..	1531	William Harris	..	1758
Richard White	..	1540	Robert Speed	..	1762
Thomas Stempe	..	1554	William Henry		
William Walker	..	1557	Reynell		1786
*John Merick	..	1570	William Blair	..	1810
William Lambert	..	1574	John Walker	..	1819
Ralph Hall ..	..	1592	Daniel George Stacey		1831
Thomas Barker	..	1595	Thomas Henry		
Charles Ryves	..	1597	Griffith		1863
Josiah White	..	1611	Robert Johnson	..	1878
Robert Polden	..	1623	Herbert Dale	..	1902

*Afterwards Bishop of Sodor and Man.

THE PARISH REGISTERS.

A search among the pages of the Parish Registers reveals a mine of interesting detail, some of which have been embodied in other parts of this book. Parish Registers were not kept in England till after the dissolution of the Monasteries. The 12th article of the injunctions signed by Cromwell, the Secretary of Henry VIII., in 1538, directs that every clergyman shall, for every Church, keep a book wherein he shall register weekly every marriage, christening, and death, any neglect being made penal. In the beginning of Elizabeth's reign this injunction was repeated.

The Registers of the Parish of Hornchurch commenced with the year 1576 (the 18th year of Queen Elizabeth), and the Overseers' and Poor Rate Book dates from 1655. Some of the pages are written in a beautiful copper-plate style, indicative of the period, or periods, when hand-writing was considered a real accomplishment. Many of the entries are curious and interesting, as shewing the customs and practices of by-gone generations.

84

The following are some of the earliest entries :—

BAPTISMS.

1576 :—Elizabeth Shunck filia Richardi 15 die mensis.
Juna Trunssell, 20 Feb.
Joh'n Thorowgood, fils Francis 2 Sept.
Elizabeth Leggatt filia Joh'n 7 Oct.
1582—January 29 :—Thomas Lanckfield, son of Thomas, by sprinkling with water adopted into the number of the Sons of God.
1584, March 20 :—Susan and Elizabeth Wylcocke, by sprinkling with water were admitted into the Church.
1603, April 17 :—Joan March, borne in ye Church porche.
1626, July 20 :—Thomas Painter, borne in a barn in the South end.
1633, June 29 :—Peter Webb, born at Durifalls.

MARRIAGES.

1576   Augustus Wakefield to Jane (Bruar) 20 Feb.
1576   Thomas Huffe to Susanna Mathye, 6 May.
,,   William Mall to Elizabeth Reade, 23 Sept.
,,   Laurence Glover to Katherine Cheese.
,,   John Hurrell to Johanna Sawnders.

BURIALS.

1576 :—John Blackmore Junr., Jan.
,,   George Bryght.
,,   John Jonson, son of Peter.
1595 :—Foster, a Chrisom* female of Richard of Hutchins.
1598 :—Ralphe Hale, Master of Artis, a right Godly Minister of Hornchurch.
1607 :—A poore vagrant boy from Mr. Hudson's of Suttons.
1642 :—Margaret Wilson, wife of George, vagabond.

Overseers' and Poor Rate Books.

The following quaint entries appear in these books :—

1670 :—Ordered at the monthly meeting this sixth day of March 1670, that the Widow Aylet, in consideration of her looking after Goodman Pool's arme, haveing a soare thereon, shall have paid to her by the present Overseers the sum of 10s.
1673 :—Paid to Daniell Chalke for cureing Mason's wife of a soor throat and knee 4s. 6d.
1679 :—Paid to Goodwife King for bread and beer at the Buryall of Wid. Elkin 2s. 6d.
1680 :—6th day of December 1680 :—
To the Doctor for phisqe for James Smith 2s.
To his reliefe at 3 times since the last month day 7s.
For a coffin for him 7s. 6d.
For fflanell to bury him in 3s. 3d.

* Baptised infants, who died within a month after their birth, were formerly shrouded in the white cloth (chrisom) put on the head at baptism, and were therefore called chrisoms.

For his buriall paid to Mr. Wells 16d. and to John Langley for half pay 12d.

For beer, fire and tobacio at his buriall 3s. 4d.

For bread at the buriall and the cheese 4s. 3d.

1685, April 6th:—To the reliefe of Goodwife Harrod when her shoulder was out of Joynt 5s.

1707, October:—Paid Francis Chesshire for worke done at ye Almshouss where Gooddy White lives 13s. 2d.

1707, October:—For a Pair of breeches for Philemon Brown 3s.

1708, April:—Paid Gooddy Baker for nursing Gooddy Bones 5 weeks 7s. 6d.

1712, June 2:—For mend. Offin boy Breeches, 1d.

1717, March 4:—For mending ye pump 5s.

1747, Aug. 2:—Money spent att the White Hart on acc't of the Vestry £1 11s. 6d.

1765, June:—Paid to the Trusts of the Turnpikes £1 5s.

1787, Dec. 10:—For dipping Thos. Brown in salt water, carriage and expenses 10s.

1828, December 9:—Thos. Biggs—5 Children—Petitions for relief of a smock frock for his son, being much distressed for apparel:—Granted a smock frock, having a large family of small children.

1829, Nov. 20:—Frank Baily's wife—4 children—Petitions for a pair of shoes for herself:—Refused, but allowed 1B. Potatoes.

1831:—Dec. 13:—John Ritch—7 children—applys for piece of Calico for the family, and some relief for the children:—Granted 8 yards for the children and 2 lbs. Bacon, but his character a very great drunkard.

VESTRY ENTRIES:—

1794:—It was ordered in Vestry that the keepers of public houses should not allow drinking in their houses on Saturday nights or on Sundays.

1863:—April 6, Easter Monday:—We do choose and appoint Thomas Hampshire to be pew opener, sexton, beadle and sydesman to the churchwardens for the year ensuing, and also Dame Hampshire to be pew opener for the year ensuing.

We do choose and appoint Mr. Frederick Jenvey to be Schoolmaster of Mrs. Aylett's Free School for the year ensuing.

SOUTH HORNCHURCH CHAPEL.

At South Hornchurch there is a Chapel of Ease to St. Andrew's Church. This was built in 1864 during the incumbency of the Rev. T. H. Griffith, a chancel being added about 18 years later, the gift of the Rev. Robert Johnson and Mrs. Helme.

A lay reader conducts the ordinary services of the

chapel, Mr. J. T. Attwooll, the present lay reader.
having acted in that capacity for over twenty years,
He was appointed by the Bishop of St. Albans (Dr.
Festing), in July, 1896, as lay reader for the parish of
Hornchurch, and was placed in charge of the chapel
by the Rev. Robert Johnson.

Mr. W. Cutler is chapel warden, and the sidesmen
are :—Messrs. J. T. Bradley, J. Cracknell, H. J. Harris,
J. Holbrook, E. Rust, G. Seeley and W. Smith.

NONCONFORMITY IN HORNCHURCH.

Hornchurch had its Nonconformist stalwarts as far
back as the 16th century. Mr. Terry, in his " Memories
of Old Romford," refers to one, John Leche, who was
again and again brought before the Archdeacon's
Tribunal for offences against the Act of Uniformity.
This man was a schoolmaster at Hornchurch, and the
principal charge against him was that he catechised
and preached in his own house, many persons besides
his own family being present every Sabbath. Leche
confessed that " he dothe catechise to his familie and
schollers in his house, and others do resort, but not by
his means."

At another time it is alleged against him " that he
oppenlie preachethe, usinge it for the manner of catechisinge ; to the which catechisinge great companie
do resort, he being not licensed thereto."

In 1587 it is further recorded that at another visitation
of the Archdeacon the following charge was made
against Leche :—" We finde and presente that on Whit
Sondaie last, being the 4th of June, we beinge com-
manded by Mr. Vichare, being at service, to goe abroad
and command men to come to service, that we found
John Leche in his private house, at an exercise, with
as greate, or rather greater, assembly than was in the
church at owre departure from the church."

Leche was eventually exccmmunicated by the Vicar
of Hornchurch, and he removed to Rcmford.

In looking through the parish registers I came across

Photo, Fred Gandon.]   HIGH   STREET.   [By permission of Luffs, Hornchurch.

the following curious entry, which would appear to refer to this same John Leche :—

" Feb. 13 1596 :—John Leech hath a Lycence to eat flesh in Lent for himselfe, his wife, hys wyves mother & hys daughter by the testymony of Richard Palmer doctor in physick."
Registered in ye presence of Nicholas Hare, Churchwarden.

A Chained Bible.

A charge was also brought before the Archdeacon's Court in September, 1577, against one George Thorogood, for nonconformist practices. The case against him having been proved, the sentence of the judge was : " That he shall by a byble of the largest volume ; and Mr. Foxes last bookes of monuments ; the which must be fastened with lokes and cheynes upon deskes within the church of Hornchurch, at the discretion of the vicare and the churchwardens, at the charges of the same Thorogood, before the next anniversary."

Although there were doubtless many adherents to nonconformity in its several forms in our village from the time of Leech right through the 17th and 18th centuries, the members of the various denominations in all probability met together in private houses, or in some semi-public way, as I can find no mention of any special building being exclusively used by them for public worship until about eighty years ago. About the year 1835 the pretty little wooden fronted house, known as the " Hollies," in North Street, was a Nonconformist Chapel, or at any rate was used for that purpose. This was followed some years later by a small mission room in a yard, at the rear of what is now the Bank buildings, in High Street. That building was used by various denominations from time to time, and was more latterly occupied by a branch of the Plymouth Brethren.

In 1882 the Baptist church in North Street was opened, and this was for many years the principal Nonconformist place of worship in the village, members of other denominations being welcomed there. Many of these were Congregationalists, and eventually they became so numerous that the need arose for a place of worship of their own, and in 1909 the Congregational Church in Nelmes Road, Emerson Park, was opened.

The formation and progress of the Baptist and Congregational Churches in Hornchurch are set out in the following chapters :—

The Baptist Church.

Prior to 1877 a little band of Baptists met together for worship in the small Mission Hall off the High Street, and on November 1 of that year a committee of management was formed, with Mr. Alexander Brewster as secretary, and Mr. John Abraham as treasurer, to advise upon the expediency of forming a Baptist Church in Hornchurch. On February 1, 1878, the Church Fellowship was duly formed, 14 persons signing the church roll. From this small beginning the Fellowship increased to such an extent that in the year 1882 it was found necessary to provide a more commodious and convenient place of worship. A site in North Street having been presented by Mr. John Abraham, of the Mill, Upminster, a building with accommodation for 220 was erected thereon. The memorial stone was laid on July 18th, 1882, at which ceremony the late Rev. Charles Haddon Spurgeon, of the Metropolitan Tabernacle, the most famous Baptist preacher and orator of that day, was the principal speaker. The following extract from the Essex Times of July 19th, 1882, gives an account of the ceremony :—

" Yesterday was a great day at Hornchurch for the local Nonconformists. It was the day set apart for the ceremony of laying the Memorial Stone of a Baptist Chapel. Mr. Henry Holmes placed his Park—Grey Towers—at the disposal of the promoters. Service was held at 3 o'clock, the Rev. C. H. Spurgeon speaking from a waggon, in which were also the Rev. J. M. Stevens, Mr. E. Dyer and Mr. H. Joslin, J.P. About 1,500 people listened to the discourse. At the close of the Service, the friends gathered on the site of the new Chapel in North Street, where Mr. John Abraham proceeded to lay the Memorial Stone."

On the afternoon of Thursday, September 21st, 1882, the newly built church was opened for divine service, when the Rev. A. G. Brown, of the East London Tabernacle, took the service and preached the first sermon. In the evening Mr. William Olney presided over a public meeting, and was supported by the Rev. A. M. Carter, Rev. F. Sweet, Mr. John Abraham and Mr. J. Templeton.

On December 11, 1882, the members of the Fellowship met to be inaugurated as a Baptist Church, the Pastor in charge being the Senior Student of Spurgeon's College, Mr. E. Dyer.

A schoolroom was erected at the rear of the church in March, 1885.

In April, 1890, Mr. Henson came to the church as the first settled Pastor, and after his removal to Stratford in June, 1891, there was no pastor in charge until April, 1894, when the Rev. Arthur Holden accepted the pastorate and continued until September, 1899.

In November, 1899, under the rights of the Trust Deeds, the church opened its fellowship to christians of other denominations. This was done in order to welcome those Nonconformists who, coming to reside in the parish, had no church of their own denomination nearer than Upminster or Romford.

In January, 1900, the Rev. F. Morris became the Pastor, and on his removal to Stapleton was followed by the Rev. Peter Miller, M.A., who was appointed in January, 1905, and, after a ministry extending over eleven years, removed in September, 1916, to Kimbolton, Huntingdon.

Of the student pastors who have had ministerial charge here are the Rev. E. Dyer (Southend), D. Hiley (Upper Norwood), and J. Gard (Guernsey).

The church was enlarged in 1903, and has seating accommodation for 270. It is free from debt, and has freehold land upon which both a church and schools could be built, giving double the present accommodation.

The present deacons and officers of the church are as follows :—Deacons : Messrs. E. D. Alley, W. Alliston, A. Ferguson, H. J. Major, F. W. Thompson and R. J. Tippin. Church Secretary : Mr. F. W. Thompson. Treasurer, Mr. H. J. Major.

The Congregational Church.

In 1905 the need of a Congregational Church began to be felt by the members of that denomination resident in Hornchurch, who, for lack of a place of worship of their own, had hitherto attended one or other of the places of worship in the village and neighbourhood. On the 2nd October of that year a meeting was held at the " Acacias," Herbert Road, Emerson Park, the residence of Mr. S. Cranfield Jenkinson. At that meeting it was decided to form a church in the neighbourhood, and on Sunday, May 13th, 1906, in a small schoolroom at " Cosy Cot," Ernest Road, were held the first services in connection with the Hornchurch Congregational Church. The services were taken by the Rev. Ira Boseley, late Chaplain to H.M. Forces. The room was only capable of accommodating about 40 persons, and it was obvious from the first that larger accommodation would have to be found as early as possible. As the outcome of this initial undertaking, a properly constituted church was formed on June 15, 1906, which was afterwards affiliated to the London Congregational Union, and in the following October the building in Berther Road, now known as Gladstone House, was acquired for the services, with accommodation for 90 persons, and here the work was carried on until September, 1909.

Early in that year it was considered that the time was ripe for the erection of a permanent building. A site was therefore obtained in Nelmes Road, the cost of which was defrayed by Mr. Thomas Dowsett, of Southend-on-Sea, and the present building, with seating accommodation for 230 persons, was erected at a cost of about £800. On July 17, 1909, the ceremony of laying memorial stones was performed. The stones were four in number and were laid by the Rev. Richard Nicholls, Mr. Thomas Dowsett (son of the donor of the site), Mr. Joseph Goodman, of Woodford Green, and Mr. Tom Hosgood, of Hackney.

On the 23rd September, 1909, the church was formally opened, and the first service held, on which occasion the sermon was preached by the Rev. D. Ewart James,

M.A., of Southend ; the opening services being continued on the following Sunday, when special sermons were preached by the late Rev. R. Wardlaw Thompson, B.A., D.D.

The building was at first designated a Lecture Hall, provision being made, when acquiring the site, for a church of much more imposing proportions, and it is intended to erect such a building whenever the needs of the district require it.

The Rev. H. J. Cubitt, B.D., of Romford, was actively associated with the movement in its initial stages, and was appointed pastor in charge at the first properly constituted church meeting, held on the 29th June, 1906, when the following Committee of Management was elected :—Messrs. J. Bauckham, C. J. Beharell, R. Guymer, G. Harvey, Sen., J. Johnson, A. J. Mills, W. S. Smith, and W. C. Vince. Mr. S. Cranfield Jenkinson was appointed church secretary, and continued in that office until January, 1913, when he was succeeded by Mr. A. C. Williams.

Mr. Cubitt continued as pastor in charge until his removal from Romford in the spring of 1907. The Rev. George Stewart, of Woodford, then took charge for a few months, and was followed in October, 1907, by the Rev. Richard Nicholls, ex-Chairman of the Lancashire Congregational Union, who carried on the work until October, 1912.

It will be of historical interest to record here the events which led up to the building of the church, and the connection of Mr. Dowsett with it. He and Mr. Jenkinson had been associated as Deacons at Cliff Town Congregational Church, Southend-on-Sea, and when Mr. Dowsett heard from his former colleague of the needs of Hornchurch, he at once showed his practical sympathy by offering to provide the site. But while the negotiations were proceeding for acquiring the ground, he was taken ill and died. He had, however, taken steps to ensure his free gift to Hornchurch. The site in the first instance was conveyed to the Rev. C. H. Vine, of Ilford, Mr. S. C. Jenkinson and Mr. W. Smith as trustees for the church, and was subsequently transferred to the London Congregational Union.

The first Deacons appointed were :—Messrs. James Bauckham, G. E. Draycott, A. Humphreys, Senr., S. C. Jenkinson, A. J. Mills, F. W. Shackell and F. J. Stradwick.

The Rev. J. Benson Evans, who formerly held Pastorates at Haverfordwest, Ramsgate and Croydon, is now Pastor, having commenced his ministry in May, 1913. The present deacons and officers of the church are :—

Mr. G. E. Draycott, Deacon.

Mr. James Bauckham, Deacon and Treasurer.

Mr. Arthur J. Mills, Deacon and Financial Secretary.

Mr. Albert C. Williams, Deacon and Churoh Secretary.

Plymouth Brethren.

There are in Hornchurch two branches of the religious community known as Plymouth Brethren, one of which has its place of worship at Billet Lane Hall, at the High Street end of Billet Lane, and the other at Suttons Hall, Suttons Lane.

THE ELEMENTARY SCHOOLS.

Our village schools indicate, as much as anything, the growth of the neighbourhood. The small building next to the Chaplaincy, recently used by the Church Lads' Brigade as a Drill Hall, was at one time the only elementary school in the village, and served to accommodate boys, girls and infants.

In 1855 the schools and schoolhouse fronting on North Street were built, by subscription, on a site presented by the Warden and Fellows of New College, Oxford, for the girls and infants, the boys still continuing to occupy the old building.

In 1886 a School Board was formed for Hornchurch, its first members being :—Colonel Henry Holmes (chairman), Messrs. T. W. Wedlake, Edward Blewett, Alfred R. Gay and Benjamin Kirkman. On the death of Mr. Kirkman, Mr. Thomas Gardner was elected in his place and, on the resignation of Colonel Holmes in 1895, became Chairman of the Board. Owing to the rapid growth of the neighbourhood, it was found that the accommodation was again insufficient for the needs of the village, and, as a consequence, the new school buildings at the rear of those fronting on North Street were built by the School Board, and completed in 1902, for the accommodation of 200 boys and 200 girls, leaving the whole of the other buildings for the infants, and abandoning altogether the old school on the top of Church Hill.

A stone tablet on the new school buildings is inscribed as follows :—

Hornchurch Board Schools.
Erected 1902.
Thomas Gardner, Esq., J.P., C.C., Chairman.
Alfred R. Gay, Vice-Chairman.

Dick Bonnett
Alfred Death } Members.
John Ferguson

Architect,
S. J. Adams, M.S.I.,
Southend-on-Sea

William Smith,
Clerk.

Builders,
F. & C. Davey,
Southend-on-Sea.

Mr. F. Edwards is Head Master, Miss E. A. Spragg Head Mistress of the Girls' School, and Miss M. Jones, Head Mistress of the Infants' School.

These Elementary Schools are, by common consent, amongst the best in this, or any other county, and it was wisely provided in the building scheme that, whenever it might become necessary, the school building could be enlarged to double its size without interfering in any way with the present structure. It contains, in addition to the ordinary classrooms, spacious manual instruction workshops, and cookery and laundry workrooms, where boys and girls in the upper classes of the senior divisions receive instruction in these special subjects.

There are also excellent school gardens, which are cultivated by the scholars, under the tuition of the Head Master.

The School Board also took over the Infant School on lease from the Vicar and Church Wardens of Hornchurch for the time being, for elementary school purposes during the customary school hours of every weekday, and for night school purposes three evenings in every week. At all other times it is at the disposal of the Vicar and Churchwardens for Sunday School and other parochial uses, and, up to the date of the erection of the Parish Council Offices in Billet Lane, in 1915, the Parish Council habitually met there.

By virtue of the Education Act of 1902, the powers and duties connected with elementary schools devolved upon the County Councils throughout the Kingdom, except in certain boroughs and urban districts, and the Essex County Council became the governing body for our local schools.

The present School Managers under the County Council are :—Mr. Thomas Gardner (chairman), Mr. Alfred R. Gay (Vice-chairman), Mrs. Gardner, Miss May, Rev. Herbert Dale, Messrs. E. Lambert, H. B. Ayres, C. H. Baker, A. Poupart, and Mr. Herbert J. Goodwin (clerk).

In addition to the Village Schools, the Managers have under their control the schools at South Hornchurch, Harold Wood, and Park Lane.

South Hornchurch School,

of which Mr. H. J. Harris, A.C.P., F.R.H.S., is Head Master, is situated in Blacksmith Lane, South Hornchurch. It was built in 1899, with accommodation for 150, and in 1912 was enlarged to accommodate 224 scholars. There is a large garden connected with this school consisting of flower borders and vegetable plots, cultivated by 20 of the elder scholars under the supervision of the Headmaster.

Park Lane School, North-West Hornchurch.

Mr. G. C. Eley, J.P., is Head Master of Park Lane School, Miss M. Beard Head Mistress of the Girls' School, and Miss E. G. Gibbs Head Mistress of the Infants' School.

This School was erected in 1893, at a cost of £4,000, and was enlarged in 1907-8, the present accommodation being for 609 children. A site has been purchased for a new Boys's School, but the building has been postponed until after the war.

Harold Wood School

was opened August, 1886, for the accommodation of 85 children, and was enlarged in 1902 to accommodate

207 children. School gardens are cultivated by the children, under the supervision of the Head Master, Mr. Thomas Rose.

THE PARISH COUNCIL.

The Local Government Act of 1894, commonly known as the Parish Councils Act, provided that every village could have its local parliament. That Act gave local popular control concerning the acquisition of land for public purposes, more especially for Allotments, and in matters relating to charities, roads and rights of way, public lighting, etc., etc.

Prior to the passing of this Act local affairs in Hornchurch had been governed by the Vestry.

On December 17th, 1894, the first election of a Parish Council for Hornchurch was held, and was very hotly contested. There were many aspirants for first Council honours, and the various candidates had much to say of themselves and their qualifications for Council work. Although Parish matters are supposed to be conducted strictly on non-party lines, two hostile camps immediately came into being, and many were the hard knocks of a wordy sort given and received. Then, as now, the villagers managed to get a good deal of amusement out of their local affairs, and humour entered largely into the contest. I am able to reproduce a facsimile of one of the electioneering appeals, and also a rhyme with an alliterative title by the village poet of that day, setting out the virtues of his side. This was answered by the opposite camp with another effusion in which alliteration was conspicuous, the heading being :—

"A Peculiar Pertinent Parody upon a Rambling Rhyming Rigmarole."

This brought a still further rejoinder with the following clever title :—

"Hornchurch Fairish Council"
or
A Reflective Relevant Rejoinder
To the Author of
A Rambling Rhyming Rigmarole
upon
A Peculiar Pertinent Parody.

FORECAST OF THE

HORNCHURCH PARISH COUNCIL

ELECTION.

A Rambling Rhyming Rigmarole
WHICH
HE WHO RUNS MAY READ.

P *stands for* **PAXON** *and* **PLAYLE**, *that is clear,*
A *for* "**ALF**" **NORRIS**, *who to speak does not fear.*
R *stands for* **RAYMENT** *a* WORKING MAN *sound.*
 I *for* INTEGRITY *in* **BAKER** *is found.*
S *stands for* **STONE**, *who is* SOLID *I ween,*
H *is for* **HORNCHURCH**, *where a* **WIN(D)MILL** *is seen.*

C *stands for* **COMPTON**, *if he lose not his breath*
O *n the* COUNCIL *he'll shine with his colleague who's* **DEATH**
U *stands for* "UNDAUNTED" **FERGUSON**, *who*
N *ow ranks as a* CHAMPION OF LABOR *most true.*
C *stands for* COURTESY, *and this I must say*
 I *n* **TURNER** *you'll find it as true as the day.*
L *stands for* **LITTLE**, *and* LAST, *there is* **JACKSON**,

And to finish my rhyme,

I sign myself

SAXON.

HORNCHURCH,
  DEC. 1894

Printed and Published by WILSON & WHITWORTH LTD., Romford and Brentwood.

I should like to have reproduced all these rhymes, but in some of their lines they were far from complimentary, and, in fact, bordered on the libellous. The "Scribe" of those days was by no means merciful.

The first Council consisted of :—Mr. Henry Compton, Chairman ; Messrs. Charles Henry Baker,* Dick Bonnett, Alfred Death, John Ferguson, William Jackson, John Little, Alfred James Norris, Walter Paxon, Frederick William Playle, George Rayment, John Stone and Joseph Turner.

The first meeting of the new Council was held in the Girls' Schoolroom, North Street, on Monday, December 31st, 1894.

The Village Pump.—One of the matters which engaged the attention of the new Council in its earlier days was the Village Pump, which, alas, had fallen into disuse for lack of a handle. After lengthy discussion it was decided to lay the matter before Emmanuel College, Cambridge, which owned the piece of land on which the pump stood, immediately in front of the present Drill Hall. The College decided to erect a new pump in place of the old one, and this was accordingly done.

We have it on the authority of a popular modern song that in another village, on the occasion of the coming of age of the squire's son :—

> "To celebrate the day in a proper sort of way,
> They shoved another handle on the pump."

But that treatment had no sort of attraction for our early Councillors, for it was found, after the new pump had been duly installed, that a handle would not answer their requirements at all, and they forthwith demanded a wheel instead. They got the wheel, and then set to work how to turn it to the best advantage. After serious deliberation they decided to use the water from the pump to water the roads. But, alas, for human calculations ! It had been overlooked that even a village pump, with a wheel at one end and a well at the other, has its limitations, and after it had been persuaded to gush forth about a watercart full of water,

* Mr. C. H. Baker has sat on the Council since its inception, and served as Chairman in 1912 and 1913.

Poll Early!

HORNCHURCH
PARISH COUNCIL ELECTION
Monday, December 17th, 1894.

INSTRUCTIONS TO VOTERS

The POLLING STATIONS will be as follows :—

No. 1. BOARD SCHOOL, PARK LANE, near Romford.
No. 2. BOARD SCHOOL, HAROLD WOOD.
No. 3. GIRLS' BOARD SCHOOL, HORNCHURCH.

The Poll will be open from 8 A.M. to 8 P.M.   PLEASE POLL EARLY.

Bring this paper with you, and place your **X** to names marked below: These are Candidates who will fairly represent you and study your interest in the Parish.

I	BAKER -	-	
2	BONNETT -	-	X
3	COMPTON	-	X
4	ORAWFORD	-	X
5	DEATH -	-	
6	FERGUSON	-	
7	FOX -	-	X
8	JACKSON -	-	X
9	JONES -	-	X
10	LITTLE -	-	X
11	NORRIS -	-	
12	PAXTON -	-	
13	PLAYLE -	-	
14	RAYMENT -	-	
15	STONE -	-	
16	TURNER -	-	
17	WINMILL -	-	X

No other mark than the **X** should be made.
The number of Councillors to be elected is THIRTEEN.
If you Vote for more than Thirteen Candidates, your Paper will be spoilt.
You cannot give more than One Vote to each Candidate.

Printed and Published by Cocksedge & Harverson, Avenue Works, Manbey Road, Stratford the supply suddenly gave out, and not for three days afterwards could it be induced to give a like quantity. This being found altogether inadequate for watering the public highway, the pump had to fall back on the functions usually expected of it.

Almost immediately after these momentous doings, someone discovered that the water from the pump was unfit for drinking purposes. The water was, thereupon, analyzed and condemned—likewise the pump. It was then ignominiously fenced in, and remains so unto this day.

Apart from the general local government of parochial affairs, the Council have carried through several important works for the betterment of the Parish, and amongst these may be mentioned the following :—

Lighting.—The Lighting and Watching Act, 1833, was adopted for the lighting of the Village Ward and the North-west Ward in 1895. In the Village Ward, 58 lamps are lit by the Council, and 94 lamps in the Northwest Ward. In both areas the lamps are unlit during June and July.

Three portions of the Parish are still unlit, *viz.* :—(1) Harold Wood, (2) Emerson Park and Great Nelmes Estates, and (3) the South Ward, south of the Midland Railway line.

Two Polls have been held as to the lighting of Harold Wood, and two as to Emerson Park, but the necessary two-thirds majority has not been obtained on any of these occasions.

Prior to the introduction of the Adoptive Acts, respecting this lighting of the two Wards mentioned, the Village Ward was partly lighted by voluntary effort, certain parishioners subscribing to a Gas Lighting Fund. The Committee which controlled this Fund handed over their lamps and lamp posts, free of cost, to the Parish Council on November 8th, 1895.

Allotments.—The Council control four fields of Allotments, two in the South Ward and two in the North-west. These Allotments are all self-supporting, the total number of plots let by the Council at the present time being 166.

The Fire Brigade.—The Hornchurch Fire Brigade had its beginning in the year 1830, when a Fire Engine was purchased by the Vestry for the sum of £18 10s.

Soon after the Parish Council came into existence in 1894, they took over from the Vicar and Churchwardens a Fire Engine, which was housed at the Old Hornchurch Brewery. This was an old-fashioned Manual, manned by a Volunteer Brigade without uniforms. The engine was removed to the old Drill Hall, which stood in Billet Lane, and steps were taken to form a more efficient Brigade. It was, however, not until 1898 that a properly uniformed and equipped Brigade was formed. In that year Mr. Edgar G. Bratchell was appointed Captain, and he has retained that office to the present date.

In 1900 the Council purchased a new 22-man Manual engine from Messrs. Shand, Mason and Co., with all the necessary hose and equipment, and in 1907 a new Fire Station was built in Billet Lane, and officially opened by Mr. R. G Ward, chairman of the Council, on July 4th of that year. The Brigade is now fully equipped with all the necessary fire extinguishing appliances and apparatus, including an efficient fire escape and hose cart.

A new sub-station was built at Harold Wood in 1914, and there is also a sub-station for north-west Hornchurch at the Durham Arms, Brentwood Road ; both are provided with hose cart, hose, etc., etc.

All parts of the parish are well provided with hydrants, excepting some portions of South Hornchurch, where there are no water mains.

The following is a list of the present members of the Fire Brigade :—

Village :—Edgar G. Bratchell, Chief Officer ; H. Alabaster, Second Officer.
Firemen :—H. Fry, W. G. Axtell, C. Green, J. Mallam and A. Pill.
North-West Hornchurch :—
Firemen :—W. J. Mumford, A. Reeves, T. Flucker.
Harold Wood :—
Firemen :—H. Stokes, G. Barker.

In addition to the above named, the following mem-

bers of the Fire Brigade are serving in H.M. Forces :—
A. G. Collin, T. G. Frost, B. Lake, B. Newman, C.
Newman, R. F. Stroud, and C. H. Fancy.

The Footpaths.—The parish is well served with
footpaths, especially in the South Ward. The Parish
Council have always been particularly keen in protecting
the public rights in the matter of footpaths, and have,
on two recent occasions, enlisted the aid of the Romford
Rural District Council to enforce the right of the public
to the use of a path', once respecting the path known as
Great Gardens Farm Footpath, and again as to Haynes
Park Bridleway.

The Council have in their office a footpath map,
which is at the disposal of any ratepayer who wishes
to inspect it. A reference to this map will probably
disclose many an unexpected and useful right of way.

Council Cottages.—The Parish Council petitioned
the Romford Rural District Council to erect workmen's
dwellings in the Village Ward, under the Housing and
Town Planning Acts, and in 1913 an inquiry was held
by the Local Government Board as to the admissibility
of allowing the Rural Council to raise a loan for the
erection of eighteen houses. Sanction was eventually
obtained for this, and eighteen houses were erected in
Abbs Cross Lane, which are let at a weekly rental of
5s. 3d. each. They form one of the finest sets of
cottages of their class in the county. They are self-
supporting, and the experiment seems to be an
unqualified success.

Council Offices.—Owing to the rapid growth of the
parish, and to the increasing activities of the Council,
the need for permanent offices arose, and in 1914 a
Parish Meeting sanctioned the raising of a loan of £850
for the purpose of erecting offices and a small hall in
which the Council could meet and carry on the business
of the parish. A committee, of which Mr. F. H. Barnes
was chairman, was appointed to arrange and supervise
the work, which involved the re-roofing of the Fire
Brigade Station adjoining the offices. Building operations were commenced in April 1915, and were completed
in the following October.

Nearly the whole of the site on which the Council Offices and Fire Station stand was presented by the late Colonel Henry Holmes, of "Grey Towers."

At a meeting of the Council on May 9th, 1916, a handsome oak and morocco chair, for the use of the chairman, was presented to the Council by Mr. Alfred Norris, of Catford, one of the members of the first Parish Council in Hornchurch.

Main Drainage.—Although the drainage of the parish is outside the scope of the Council, the scheme which was eventually adopted was the outcome of their initiative. On the 26th January, 1899, a Parish Meeting was held; under the chairmanship of Mr. Thomas Gardner, at which a resolution was passed in favour of a Main Drainage Scheme for the Village Ward.* The Romford Rural District Council eventually gave effect to this resolution, and an efficient sewerage scheme put in hand, which was completed in 1902.

The Hornchurch Parish Council, as originally constituted, consisted of 13 members. This was increased to 15 in 1905—one member being added for both the Village and North West Wards.

The present Council is as under :—

Village Ward :—Messrs. C. H. Baker, A. G. Dohoo, Walter Halestrap, Alexander Ferguson and W. E. Cogar.

North-West Ward :—Messrs. W. H. Legg, Edwin Lambert, H. J. Finch and J. S. Everson.

South Ward :—Messrs. Thomas Crawford, A. E. Chaplin, and Arthur Knight.

Harold Wood Ward :—Messrs. W. J. Westaway, M. E. Ricketts and Frank Creek.

Overseers :—Messrs. W. E. Cogar, Frank Creek, Thomas Crawford and J. S. Everson.

Mr. William C. Allen is Clerk to the Council and Chief Assistant Overseer ; and Mr. W. A. Warman (now on Active Service with H.M. Forces) is junior Assistant Overseer.

* The Drainage for the N.W. Ward was installed in 1898, and that for Harold Wood in 1903.

1894 to 1896	..	Mr. Henry Compton.
1897 to 1900	..	Mr. Thomas Gardner
1901 to 1904	..	Mr. John Little
1905 to 1907	..	Mr. R. G. Ward
1908	..	Mr. A. C. Powell
1909	..	Mr. Francis H. Barnes
1910 to 1911	..	Mr. Edwin Lambert
1912 to 1913	..	Mr. Charles H. Baker
1914	..	Mr. E. A. Pearce
1915 to 1916	..	Mr. William H. Legg
1917	..	Mr. Alexander Ferguson

Romford Rural District Council.

The Hornchurch representatives on the Romford Rural District Council (who are also Guardians of the Poor) are as follows :—

* Mr. Edgar G. Bratchell	Village Ward
Mr. Thomas Crawford	Do.
Mr. Edwin Lambert	North-West Ward
Mr. A. F. Harrison	Do.
Mr. Alexander Ferguson	South Ward
Mr. D. Shuttleworth	Harold Wood Ward

THE VILLAGE NURSING FUND.

The Hornchurch Nursing Fund was established in 1897, by a grant of £52 from the amount raised by public subscription to commemorate the Diamond Jubilee of Queen Victoria. From that time onwards it has been entirely supported by voluntary contributions. It provides and maintains a qualified nurse, whose services may be obtained by the parishioners at charges which are arranged on a very moderate scale. While the Fund is primarily intended for the benefit of the poorer inhabitants, its scope is not restricted in any way, the services of the Nurse being available to all Hornchurch parishioners.

It would be impossible to overestimate the beneficent character and usefulness of this Fund, which is fully deserving of all the support which can be accorded to it.

* Mr. Bratchell was Chairman for the years 1916 and 1917.

Present Committee and Staff :—Chairman :—Rev.
Herbert Dale, M.A. Committee :—Mrs. Allen, Mrs.
Dale, Mrs. Greatorex, Mrs. Jones, Miss Keighley, Mrs.
Low, Mrs. Pailthorpe, Mrs. Saville.

Mr. and Mrs. W. E. Langridge, who for a period of
over ten years acted respectively as Hon. Treasurer
and Hon. Secretary, have been elected Life Members of
the Committee.

Hon. Treasurer :—Mr. E. Spenser Tiddeman.
Hon. Secretary :—Mrs. E. Spenser Tiddeman.
Nurse :—Miss Laura Rudland.

THE CHARITIES.

Hornchurch, owing to its antiquity, and to the
benevolent people who have lived here in the past, is
rich in charities, and at the present time very considerable sums of money are at the disposal of the trustees.
There have been several investigations into these
charities from time to time, one of which occurred in
1830, the public notice of which is here reproduced.
It is assumed that the list given thereon represented the
whole of the charities then existing. Another enquiry
took place in the year 1878. The most recent investigation was in 1911-1912, when a representative committee was appointed, and on the recommendation
of that committee an application was made to the
Charity Commissioners for a new scheme to replace
that of 1878. This application was made on Feb. 1,
1911, and on January 19, 1912, the Commissioners
sanctioned the scheme which is now in operation.
Included in that scheme are Pennant's Almshouses,
Appleton's Almshouses, and Rame's Charity Estate.

Pennant's Almshouses are situated in the High
Street, near the corner of Billet Lane. They were
bequeathed by Pierce Pennant, who was servant to
King Edward VI. and Queen Mary, and also gentleman
usher to Queen Elizabeth. His monument in Hornchurch Church is thus inscribed :—

Here lyeth buried Peerce Pennante Esquire servante to
our late soveraigne Lord Kynge Edwarde ye syxte and Queene
Mary and also one of the gentlemen ushers in ordynary the
space of two & thirtie yeres to our Soveraigne Ladie Queene

List of Charities

BELONGING TO THE POOR OF HORNCHURCH,

Examined and Reported on by Thomas Mashiter, Esq.

1830.

PENNANTS HOUSES, left by *Thomas Legatt, Esq.* as a Residence for the Poor: now occupied as a Workhouse.

THE CHURCH CHARITY consists of Two Acres of Land called *Gogneys*, and Eight Acres of Land in the Parish of Romford called *Gibbs and Perrys*, let to *Miles* and *Reynolds*, at £24 per annum. To be applied in repairing the Church.

RAMM'S, Two Houses let to *Turpin* and *Manning*, on Lease for 31 Years, at £10 per annum. To be applied in Charity as the Trustees think fit to direct.

APPLETON'S, Three Cottages and Gardens, to be let to Three poor Families, at 10s. 2d. per Annum each, they keeping the Windows in repair. The Rents to accumulate as a Fund for repairs.

DAMON'S, Two Cottages, let to *Thompson* and *Cooper*, at £11. 6s. per annum.

WEST FIELD, Two Acres of Land, let to *Samuel Benton*, at £6 per annum.
The above, DAMON'S and WEST FIELD were left by *Sybella Shoals*, to keep her Tomb in repair; the residue to be applied in Charity, as the Trustees direct.

WEDSTER'S, the Tile-kiln, at Romford, let to *Joseph Moore*, at £4 per annum.

THOMAS CLARKE, One Pound Annuity, chargeable on Ford Lodge

DAVID RICKETTS, Interest on £100 South Sea 3 per Cent. Stock

JOHN RICHARDSON, Interest on £100 3 per Cent. Reduced Stock

HANNAH RICHARDSON, Interest on £100 5 per Cent. Navy Stock

WILLIAM HIGGS, Interest on £100 3 per Cent. Consolidated Stock

BURCHET WHENNELL, One Guinea chargeable on Albyn's Farm

> The Income arising from these Charities is to be expended in Bread, to be given to the Poor of the Parish, in the Month of October, and on Saint Thomas's Day.

THOMAS PAGE, Interest on £100 5 per Cent. Navy Stock, to keep his Tomb in repair, and the remainder to be given to poor Widows in money on St. Thomas's Day.

WILLIAM ARMSTEAD, an Annuity of £6 chargeable on Lands let to *Barwell*, at Hay's Green. The purport is for the Minister to preach Two Sermons, at 10s. each, on Lady-day and Michaelmas-day. The remainder to be distributed to the Poor in Money, on those Days.

WILLIAM HIGGS, £100 in Money to be lent to Four poor Tradesmen or Farmers, for Three Years successively, without Interest.

ALICE AYLETT, an Annuity of £10 chargeable on the Estate called *Langtons*, for the purpose of teaching Ten poor Boys. The Master to be elected annually, on Easter Monday.

WILLIAM JACOBS left the Interest of £200 to be applied towards increasing the means of educating the above Ten poor Boys.

JAMES COVE placed £18 on the 29th of April, 1829, in the Romford Savings Bank, the Interest of which is to be applied to *Alice Aylett's* Charity.

EDWARD OAKLEY, a Cottage on Butt's Green, let on Lease to *G. Stevens*, at £3 per annum. To be applied in Charity, as the Trustees think fit.

JOHN BOURNE, £20. the Interest to be given to the Poor, as Trustees think fit; paying the Clerk or Sexton 2s. 6d. for keeping his Grave in repair and cleaning the Head and Foot Stone.

3r. 26p. of LAND, given by Commissioners of Enclosure, and let to *Staines*, at 15s. per annum. The Money to be applied in Charity, as the Trustees think fit.

1r. 6p. of ditto, given by Commissioners of Enclosure.

JOHN MASSU, Esq. £1000. East India Stock, to be vested in Three Trustees to be chosen by the Vestry, and the Dividends to be applied to Ten poor Men who have never received any Parochial Relief.

HYDE'S CHARITY, to bind-out poor Children Apprentices, is managed by Nine Trustees of Horachurch, Romford, the Vicar of Hornchurch, and Chaplain of Romford.

ROGER REEDE'S ALMS HOUSES for decayed Tradesmen, is managed by Trustees appointed by a Master in Chancery.

☞ **N.B.** Her Majesty's Commissioners for Charities, and Education of the Poor of England and Wales, have appointed their Inspector to enquire into the Accounts of the several Charities above-named, on TUESDAY, 18th JUNE, at 12 o'Clock, Noon, at the SUNDAY SCHOOL, at which the Rate-Payers are particularly requested to attend.

H

Elizabeth which said Peerce deceased the thirtethe daye of November in the yere of our Lorde God 1590 being of the age of threscore and tenne yercs.

The almshouses originally consisted of four cottages. There are at present eight tenements, occupied by five widows and three married couples. A stone in front of the building bears the following inscription :—

PENNANT'S ALMSHOUSES

1597

Restored by Thos. Mashiter, Esq.

1837.

Appleton's Almshouses are on the south side of the High Street. They consist of three small houses, left by Henry Appleton in 1587, and are at present occupied by two married couples and Mrs. Mary Ann Smith (widow), our oldest inhabitant, who is in her 91st year.

Rame's Charity Estate consists of two houses in Church Street, which were bequeathed by Anthony Rame in 1621.

These are let, and the proceeds, after paying for up-keep and repairs, go towards the funds of the Consolidated Charities.

The Charities are administered by six trustees, appointed by the Parish Council, and one ex-officio trustee, the Vicar of Hornchurch for the time being. The present trustees are :—Rev. Herbert Dale (Chairman), Messrs. W. H. Legg, A. J. Thompson, J. S. Everson, Frank Creek, Arthur Knight and C. H. Baker, Honorary Clerk and Vice-Chairman.

In addition to the parochial charities there is one charity known as "**Whennell's and Bearblock's Charity**," which is purely an ecclesiastical charity. The capital is invested in Consols, the proceeds of which are expended at the discretion of the Vicar in prizes, books, apparatus, and furniture for the Sunday School. The income of this Charity is now about £10 per annum.

ROGER REEDE'S CHARITY.

Although many of the charities concerned in the foregoing chapter have been of a very benevolent character, the most noble of all local charities is that known as Roger Reede's Charity. This is not entirely a Hornchurch Charity, its benefits being shared by the three parishes of Romford, Hornchurch, and Dagenham. It was founded A.D. 1483, by the will of Roger Reede for the benefit of five poor men "fallen in estate," and the widows of such men if married at the time of their election, no person being qualified to any benefit of the Charity who has received parochial relief or assistance.

The charity is regulated by a scheme of the Court of Chancery, confirmed by an Order dated 10th December, 1825, and varied by an Order of the same Court dated 30th April, 1860, and further, by order of the Charity Commissioners (in virtue of the Charitable Trusts Acts 1853 to 1887), sealed on the 29th April, 1890.

By the present regulations there are six almshouses, providing accommodation for six married couples. Each almsman receives an allowance of £39 a year, payable quarterly, with a suit of clothes annually, and a great coat when necessary ; and his wife receives annually a new gown and petticoat, and, during her widowhood, £33 per annum, and residence in her late husband's house. Coals are supplied as required, and a doctor at an annual stipend of £10 10s. attends the pensioners in cases of illness, any extra expense being allowed for nursing, special nourishment or medical comforts ordered by him.

Out of the surplus income a sum of £30 (sometimes more) is appropriated in distributing cloaks, overcoats, blankets, and flannel at the discretion of the trustees, when other occasions of the charity will permit, amongst the neighbouring poor of the parishes of Hornchurch, Romford, and Dagenham. What remains of the surplus income, after the above payments, is retained by the trustees as an accumulating fund to pay the cost of dilapidations of the almshouses and any other part of the charity estates.

One almsman is appointed ruler at the almshouses, and receives £4 annually, in addition to his pension. His duties are to keep the key of the gate, and report any circumstance which has occurred relative to the conduct of the alms people, or anything about which he requires advice from the trustees.

When an almsman dies a meeting is called of the trustees on the fourth Tuesday subsequent to the decease, when a successor is elected by the trustees present. Notice of this, stating the day of the election, has to be given or posted at the church of the parish, from which the vacancy is to be filled, on the following Sunday after the burial of the deceased.

In the opinion of the Charity Commissioners the Charity is non-parochial.

The endowment consists of land to the amount of about 140 acres, and sundry cottages and house property.

The almshouses are situated in North Street, Romford. They were rebuilt in 1784 and again in 1896.

The trustees (or feoffees, as they were originally called) must not be more than sixteen, or less than five in number. The present trustees and the dates of their appointment are as under :—

1884. George Palmer Hope, Esq., The Grange, Havering.
1902. Sir Thomas Neave, Bart., Dagnam Park, Romford.
1902. Sir Frederick Green, Hainault Lodge, Hainault.
1905. Sir Montague Cornish Turner, Bedfords, Havering.
1905. Rev. Herbert Dale, Vicar of Hornchurch.
1905. Thomas Gardner, Esq., Duryfalls, Hornchurch.
1905. James Robert Robertson, Esq., Fairkytes, Hornchurch.
1912. The Right Hon. Lord O'Hagan, Pyrgo Park, Havering.
1912. Major Henry Jessop Stone, Lower Bedfords, Havering.
1912. Rev. George Milner Bell, Vicar of Romford.
1912. Rev. Clement Charles Harrison, Vicar of Dagenham.
1912. Herbert Edward Ingle, Esq., Merrielands, Dagenham.
       The Clerk and Receiver is Mr. F. J. Hunt, Romford.

The Will of Roger Reede.

The will of Roger Reade was dated 15th February, 1482, and was so quaintly worded that I give an extract dealing with that part of it in which the Almshouses are bequeathed, viz. :—

"My place, new built, in Joy's Mead, otherwise called Hoo Croft, to remain to the behoof of five poor men, such as I, the aforesaid Roger, shall leave therein and ordain to be put therein, and afterwards, as they decease, to be chosen by the advice of my executors, and of myne feoffees, and of such a person or persons as shall

have a rule under my said Feoffees. And that those
persons so by them chosen be no blasphemers of the
name of Almighty God. And that as far forth as they
may understand and know as they will answer before
Almighty God and in discharging of their own conscience.
And that they put in no common beggars, but such as
have been of good governance and be fallen in poverty.
Also my will is that which of the aforesaid five poor
men be most saddest and wisest and so be known by
the discretion of my Feoffees that he have his dwelling
in the Great Hall place in Joy's Mead before rehearsed
and therein all the aforesaid five poor men to keep their
commons, if they can so agree, and to be taken among
them as a ruler, to see them guided, and to see the
reparations kept all in general at their costs paying
the quit rent of the said Mead and Housings and none of
them be not absent from their dwelling place past a
day and a night without license of their ruler for the
time being. And also the said ruler see them, and
each of them, once in the day, either in the church or in
their dwelling, busy in their prayers and every Sunday
and holy day and other days when they come to the
church, to be about my sepulchre and of my wife's,
there praying for my soul and for my wife's soul, and
for all my good friends' souls. And also my will is
that the five poor men after they be chosen in, wed no
wives, but keep themselves sole."

THE DRILL HALL.

In the early days of the Rifle Volunteers the local
Company of the 15th Essex used the small schoolroom
on the top of Church Hill as their Drill Hall.

About the year 1866 a Drill Hall was erected by public
subscription in the Billet Lane, on or near the site of
the present Council Offices, and there public entertainments, meetings and social events of the village
were held.

After the formation of the Hornchurch Company
(No. 9) of the Essex Artillery Volunteers, Major Henry
Holmes built and presented to the Company the Drill
Hall now standing in the High Street. This Hall was

formally opened on the 21st November 1892. It is 85 feet long by 45 feet wide, and it originally had a gravelled floor. The cost of the Hall was about £500.

As Hornchurch is without a **Village Hall,** the Drill Hall is used for most of the big public meetings, social and political, as well as for balls, concerts and other public functions. It may not be out of place to suggest that the erection of a Public Hall would probably be one of the most fitting ways of commemorating Peace, whenever that happy event may take place.

THE VOLUNTARY MILITARY AND SEMI-MILITARY ORGANIZATIONS AND MOVEMENTS IN HORNCHURCH.

Hornchurch has always been prominent in the various voluntary military, and semi-military movements which have arisen from time to time. In 1860, within a year of the establishment of the National Rifle Association, a Company of Rifle Volunteers was formed in Hornchurch, which was attached to the 15th Essex Rifle Volunteer Corps.

Some few years later, in 1882, a Battery (No. 9) of the First Essex Artillery Volunteers was formed, which for a considerable period had a very successful career. That Battery has now ceased to exist.

The Rifle Volunteer Corps eventually became H. Company of the 1st Volunteer Battalion Essex Regiment, and when the South African War broke out seven men of the Company were chosen for active service, viz. :—Sergeant Walter Halestrap, Corporal H. Alexander, and Privates F. Chester, H. Chester, J. Cole, H. Halestrap and T. Tarling ; all of whom returned after the war, with the exception of Private F. Chester, who died in Pretoria on 14th July, 1900.

When the Volunteers were superseded by the Territorial Force in 1908, our local Company became part of the 4th Battalion Essex Regiment, and at the outbreak of the Great War the Company was called up for Home Service, under the command of Major H. H. Slade. Afterwards practically all the men volunteered for

Foreign Service, and served first in Gallipoli, and afterwards in France and elsewhere.

THE NATIONAL RESERVE.—In 1912 the National Reserve came into being, with the object of utilizing the services of men who had completed their period of service in the Navy, Army, and Auxiliary Forces. An appeal to Hornchurch men to join this Reserve resulted in the formation of a strong Company, which, at the time of the outbreak of hostilities in 1914, was well and efficiently organized, and all the men of the Company who were of military age were called to the colours.

CHURCH LADS' BRIGADE AND CADETS.—The Hornchurch Company of the Church Lads' Brigade was formed in 1903, and speedily became one of the largest and most successful Companies of the 4th Battalion St. Albans Regiment. In September, 1911, the local C.L.B. Battalion became a recognised unit of the Territorial Forces, and was designated the 2nd Chelmsford Cadet Battalion, and in June, 1914, were equipped with the infantry khaki service uniform. Early in 1917 the Battalion was affiliated to the regular Battalions of the King's Royal Rifle Corps, and now wears the uniform of that Corps. With few exceptions all the members of the Company of military age joined the regular Army during the first months of the war, and many others, who have since arrived at military age, have joined during the last three years.

THE BOY SCOUTS.—The Hornchurch Section of the Boy Scouts is attached to the 3rd Romford Troop of the Baden-Powell Boy Scouts, and while the First Sportsman's Battalion was in training at Grey Towers, and also in the earlier period of the New Zealanders' occupation of that Camp, they acted as Camp orderlies. Many of their members later joined H.M. Forces and have seen active service in the war.

CHURCH NURSING AND AMBULANCE BRIGADE.— A branch of the Church Nursing and Ambulance Brigade was formed in Hornchurch in November, 1910, and continued its activities as a Company until November, 1915. It was under the leadership of Miss Keighley and Miss May, and, with the tuition of Dr. Wagstaff, Dr. Bernard Wagstaff, Dr. Bletsoe, and Dr. Sanderson, did excellent work in the training of young women and girls in First Aid, Home Nursing, and Hygiene. The Brigade wore uniform, and several of its members have taken up definite work in nursing and massage during the war time.

War-Time Organizations.

THE VOLUNTEER TRAINING CORPS.—In 1914-15, Volunteer Training Corps were established all over the kingdom. Hornchurch formed part of the Romford and District Corps, which was attached to the Essex Volunteer Regiment, and in the earlier days of the movement supplied about 40 members to the Corps.

ESSEX CADET CORPS.—In 1916 invitations were sent to the County Educational Committees throughout the kingdom to encourage the formation of Cadet Corps in connection with the Elementary Schools. Essex was one of the first counties to adopt the suggestions put forward by the authorities. A four-company Battalion was formed for Romford and District, attached to the Essex Regiment, and bearing the title of the Cadet Battalion of the 4th Essex Regiment. Hornchurch supplied one of the Companies to this Battalion.

Many of the brave men and lads who cheerfully came out from these voluntary forces to serve their King and Country have lost their lives, or have been wounded in this gigantic struggle in various parts of the world, and their heroism and self-sacrifice will be suitably inscribed in the parish record* to be published at the conclusion of the war.

* The miltary and semi-military organizations in Hornchurch have only been very briefly described in the above chapter. I hope to be able to publish, in due course, in a book entitled ' Hornchu ch during the Great War,' the full record of their history and work extending over a period of 60 years and more particularly their magnificient service in the present war. (See announcement at the end of the book. — C. T. P.

HORNCHURCH AND DISTRICT MINIATURE RIFLE CLUB.

Hornchurch possesses one of the best open-air Rifle Ranges in the county. It adjoins Hornchurch Station (L.T. and S. Section, M.R.), and, being on ground which was formerly a gravel pit, it is partly surrounded by what are practically cliffs ; there is therefore very little fear of accident, even in the direct firing line. Through the instrumentality of Mr. J. R. Robertson this fine site was granted, free of rent, to the Club by Mr. J. E. Yerburgh and Mr. Henry Peake.

There are ranges at 25, 50 and 100 yards, all the firing points being under cover.

It was at a meeting at the Drill Hall in January, 1912, that it was decided to form a Miniature Rifle Club for the district. Mr. Thomas Gardner was elected its first President (and still retains that office), and Mr. A. G. Sibthorp was its first Hon. Secretary and Treasurer, Sergeant-Major Young being appointed Range Officer. Practice began in the following month at the Drill Hall, and in April a ladies' team was formed, with Mrs. Gardner as Hon. Secretary of that Section.

On Whit Monday, 27th May, 1912, the open-air range was inaugurated, Mrs. Gardner performing the opening ceremony, and firing the first shot, scoring a bull.

At the first annual meeting held in November, 1912, it was announced that the membership of the Club was 291, viz. :—A President, 44 Vice-Presidents, 96 ordinary members, 30 lady members, 80 of the 4th Battalion Essex Territorial Regiment, and 40 of the Church Lads' Brigade.

In September, 1913, the Annual County Prize Meeting was held on the Range.

Apart from the privileges enjoyed by the members and the general usefulness of the Club, the Range has been of real national importance during the war, for here the 1st Sportsman's Battalion went through their small-bore training in 1915, and in 1916 the men of the New Zealand Contingent stationed at Great Towers Camp had full use of the Range, and fired a series of matches with the Ladies' Team. In the same year the Upminster Platoon of the Essex Volunteer Regiment qualified at this Range for their firing tests, and in 1917 the local Company of the Cadet Battalion of the 4th Essex Regiment was granted free use of it for firing practice.

At the commencement of the war Sergeant-Major Young rejoined his old regiment, the 4th Essex, and Mr. G. M. Horey became Honorary Range Officer, and, with the assistance of Mrs. Horey—Captain of the Ladies' Team—"carried on" and made all the arrangements for the many useful purposes which the Range has served during the last three years.

Mr. C. L. Parker has acted as Hon. Secretary and Treasurer since January, 1916.

The Club is affiliated to the Society of Miniature Rifle Clubs and to the Essex County Rifle Association.

During the period of the war no less than 70 members have joined H.M. Forces. A splendid record !

THE RAILWAY.

How many of us, who are wont to cavil at the facilities afforded us by the London, Tilbury and Southend Section of the Midland Railway, would care to be subject to the railway conditions which prevailed in the middle of the last century ? Hornchurch was then served by the Eastern Union and Eastern Counties Railway, which is now the Great Eastern Railway. Romford was the nearest station, and continued to be so, until 1885, when the first section of the Barking and Pitsea Extension of the London, Tilbury and Southend Railway was opened. I recently had before me Truscott's Timetables for November of the year 1848, and a few details of the train service will perhaps be of interest to our city men, who have now the choice of Hornchurch Station, and Emerson Park and Great Nelmes Halt on the Midland Railway, and Squirrels Heath Station on the G.E.R.

In those days there were only six trains every weekday to and from London, and one train less on Sundays. The last down train started from Bishopsgate Terminus

Photo, Fred Gandon.]

SUTTONS LANE.

[By permission of Luffs, Hornchurch.

—there was then no Liverpool Street Station—at 8.30 p.m., and the last train left Romford for London at 8.44 p.m. It is somewhat surprising to learn that the journey was done, even in those far-off days, in 24 minutes, though some of the trains took as long as 51 minutes. The usual run occupied about half an hour.

There is a curious announcement at the end of the Timetable, which is as follows :—

" Post horses are in readiness at the London Terminus on the arrival of every train. Charge to any part of London, including post-boy, 10s. 6d. Post horses may also be secured at any of the principal Stations, by giving notice one day previously to the Chief Clerk of the Station where they are required."

In connection with the Romford service of trains, a " branch Coach " met one train a day, viz. :—the 5.30 p.m. from London, presumably the business man's train, which conveyed passengers to Hornchurch, Upminster, Corbets Tey, and South Ockendon. In later days the Coach service was much accelerated, and the sight of the lumbering old 'bus, which the Railway Company dignified by the name of Coach, passing through the village, will be within the recollection of quite a large number of Hornchurch folk.

In the eighties, however, all this was altered, for the L.T. and S. Railway had been concerning itself with regard to the making of a direct line from London to Southend, via Upminster, and in 1883 this took definite shape. On October 11th of that year the first turf was cut of the new Barking and Pitsea extension, with stations at Dagenham, Hornchurch, Upminster, East Horndon and Laindon. This ceremony was performed in a field close to the mill at Upminster by Mrs. Doughty Browne, the wife of the Chairman of the Company.

In less than two years from the date of this ceremony, the first section of the new extension was opened, viz. :— From Barking to Upminster, and on the 1st May, 1885, the first train steamed into Hornchurch Station. Exactly one year later, on 1st May, 1886, East Horndon Station was opened, and on 1st June, 1888, the extension through to Pitsea was completed, and Laindon Station opened.

Mr. James R. Robertson was the Resident Engineer in charge of the construction of the new line on behalf of the Railway Company.

The first section of the single branch line between Romford and Grays, viz. :—Upminster-Ockendon-Grays, was opened on 1st July, 1892, and that from Romford to Upminster on 7th June, 1893.

Emerson Park and Great Nelmes Halt on this Branch was opened on 1st October, 1909.

The Midland Railway took over the whole system of the London, Tilbury and Southend Railway on 1st January, 1912.

EMERSON PARK ESTATE.

On the occasion of the cutting of the first turf of the railway extension mentioned in the preceding chapter, there appeared in the *Daily Telegraph* a descriptive article on the locality, of which the following is an extract :—

" Lying between Brentwood on the north and Tilbury on the south is one of the prettiest parts of the county of Essex, hitherto almost unknown to the London holiday maker, for the reason that the two eastern lines of Railway have altogether avoided it. Hornchurch, more renowned for its fellmongery in ancient times than now . . . . . is still one of the quaintest towns one could wish to see, with its two straggling streets, its church bearing the insignia of its name, its gabled houses placed anywhere and everywhere the owners pleased, supremely indifferent to architectural continuity, and its general disregard for the amenities of locomotion. Those who wish to see it as it is, and as it has been for centuries, must visit it soon, for yesterday there was cut at Upminster the first turf of a railway which will bring the place within half an hour of London, and open up a new field for the speculative contractor." (*Daily Telegraph*, Oct. 12, 1883).

For a period of twelve years after this event, the old village was spared the fate foreshadowed in the concluding words of the passage above quoted. In the year 1895, Hornchurch was, however, " discovered " by Mr. William Carter, of Parkestone, Dorset, who purchased 200 acres of land originally forming part of the historic Manor of Nelmes, and 20 acres of the Manor of Lees-Gardens, including the fine old house known as **Wych Elm** now owned and occupied by Mr. Thomas W. Catherwood, and, bestowing upon it the name of Emerson Park Estate, commenced the building of modern Hornchurch. And so it came about that we have to-day in this residential estate an ideal and typical garden suburb, composed of about 280 picturesque detached villas and bungalows, with their large and beautiful gardens, many of them exceeding an acre in extent. Its four miles of roads are still unlit at night, the dwellers of Emerson Park being so appreciative of their rural surroundings that two Polls have failed to secure for this part of the parish the adoption of the Lighting and Watching Act of 1833.

Mr. W. H. C. Curtis had in his hands the development of the Estate from its inception, and when, in the year 1903, it was absorbed by Homesteads, Limited, he became the General Manager of that Company, which at the present time has similar residential estates in sixteen counties.

During the period Emerson Park has been in existence, the population of Hornchurch has nearly doubled itself, and it may safely be assumed that the development of this Estate has played a conspicuous part in bringing about this satisfactory result. Its limitation has in these days been nearly reached, most of the land having been taken up, but the growth of the parish still continues through the medium of the **Great Nelmes Estate** (already referred to in the chapter on the Manor of Nelmes), the **Rosemount Estate** in Hornchurch Road, and the **Mill Park Estate** in Suttons Lane.

THE CONSERVATIVE AND LIBERAL UNIONIST ASSOCIATION AND CLUB.

A strong consensus of Conservative conviction has always existed in Hornchurch, but prior to the formation of a Conservative Club, in Billet Lane, about 1906, there was no organisation of a permanent character for the promulgation of Conservative principles. Previously, political activity only began to become demonstrative shortly before the occurrence of a Parliamentary election, when a meeting of adherents would be convened at which a Committee was appointed to carry out the work of canvassing the electors, and generally to promote the return of the selected candidate. When the election was over, the Committee was dissolved, and political calm again supervened. But, with the appearance of the Conservative Club, more stable conditions were created. Shortly after its inauguration it was thought that the movement might be further supported and accentuated by the establishment of an organisation on a purely political basis, extended in scope so as to include Liberal Unionists as well as Conservatives. Thus the Conservative and Liberal Unionist Association came into being, with Mr. Charles Dunlop as its first President.

The operations of the two organisations—the Club and the Association—though not in conflict, were found to involve a considerable amount of overlapping. This state of things, however, was speedily remedied, and an amalgamation of the two institutions resulted, under the style of the Hornchurch Conservative and Liberal Unionist Association and Club.

As the premises in Billet Lane were of too limited a nature to afford the requisite accommodation for the increased membership, it was resolved to acquire a piece of land in North Street, on which to erect a suitable building. With this object a Company was registered, called the Hornchurch Constitutional Company, Limited. The necessary capital was subscribed, and the building completed in 1910, at a cost of £1,200.

The Directors of the Constitutional Company, Ltd., are : Messrs. W. Varco Williams, J.P., C.C., W. G. Key, E. G. Bratchell, J.P., J. A. McMullen, and R. G. Ward ; Mr. McMullen acting as Hon. Secretary, and Mr. F. Beddow as Hon. Auditor.

The Inaugural and First Annual Dinner of the Association and Club was held at the Club House on Tuesday, 13th March, 1913, at which Mr. J. A. McMullen presided.

The present officers are :—President, Mr. W. Varco Williams ; Vice-Presidents, Sir W. P. Griggs, Mr. Charles

Dunlop, Mr. J. A. McMullen, Mr. J. R. Robertson, Mr. Thomas Gardner and Mr. W. G. Key ; Trustees, Mr. F. A. Emmerson, Mr. J. W. Dunlop, Mr. J. D. Johnson ; Chairman, Major J. M. Ewing ; Vice-Chairman, Mr. C. E. Dunlop ; Hon. Secretary, Mr. A. E. Palmer ; Hon. Treasurer, Mr. A. E. Mohring.

THE LIBERAL AND RADICAL ASSOCIATION.

The Hornchurch Liberal and Radical Association was formed in 1903, its objects being the diffusion of Liberal and Radical principles, and the registration of electors. All Liberals and Radicals residing in, or connected with, the Parliamentary Division are eligible for membership.

The officers of the Association are as follows :—President, Sir J. G. Broodbank ; Vice-Presidents, Sir John H. Bethell, Bart., M.P., Sir H. H. Raphael, Bart., M.P., Sir John Simon, K.C.V.O., K.C., M.P., Baron de Forest, M.P., Percy Alden, Esq., M.P., A. Cecil Beck, Esq., M.P., C. F. G. Masterman, Esq., M.P., James Rowlands, Esq., M.P., H. M. Thornton, Esq., J.P., and Messrs. J. W. Crouch, T. A. Gawler, John Page, W. H. C. Curtis, S. C. Jenkinson, T. W. Catherwood, and F. W. Parker ; Chairman, Mr. Walter Young, LL.B., J.P. ; Treasurer, Mr. T. W. Catherwood ; Hon. Association Secretary, Mr. G. Gregg ; Hon. Club Secretary, Mr. R. F. Stroud.

The membership before the outbreak of war was about 200, but a great many of the members are now on active service, including the Club Secretary, Mr. R. F. Stroud.

There is also a junior section for youths under military age, the Hon. Secretary of which is Mr. G. H. Bradley.

For a short time the Association had an office in the High Street, but in 1911 the building, known as Gladstone House, with the land adjoining it in Berther Road, was purchased, the object being attained by a Limited Company promoted by the Association, under the title of Gladstone House (Hornchurch), Limited. In this building a great deal of work has been carried out, and the Association claims its share in the three Liberal and Radical victories at the General Elections of 1906, and January and December, 1910. The building includes a hall, in which meetings, etc., are held, also Library, Committee and Billiard rooms.

All political activity having been suspended during the war, the only functions now carried on by the Associations are of a social character, the chief of these being a series of evening social entertainments for the wounded New Zealand soldiers encamped at Hornchurch These entertainments have been carried on weekly since November, 1916.

THE ROMFORD PARLIAMENTARY DIVISION OF ESSEX.

The Romford Division of Essex, of which Hornchurch forms part, is the largest Parliamentary constituency in Great Britain. According to the census of 1911, the population was 312,864, and it is still rapidly increasing. More than one third of the population reside in Greater London, and most of the electors are employed in, or are connected with, the Metropolis ; the whole of them live in, or on the border of the greatest city of the Empire.

In 1913 the electorate was 57,882,* and this large number of electors is only empowered to send one Member to the House of Commons.

A parliamentary commission is now (1917) sitting, under the presidency of the Speaker of the House of Commons, to consider electoral reform, and, in view of possible changes in Parliamentary representation, I record here, by way of comparison, an interesting table, compiled by Mr. G. Jellis Battle, Unionist Agent for the Division, which shows some astonishing inequalities in Parliamentary representation :—

15 English Boroughs show a combined electorate of ..	54,480
10 Metropolitan Boroughs	53,901
8 County Divisions	54,950
12 Scottish Constituencies	53,291
8 Welsh ,, ...	53,635
15 Irish ,, ...	57,595

It will be seen that in all the above named instances

* At the present time (1917) the electorate is 62,878.

the total electorate is less than in the Romford Division ; and it is further pointed out that a vote in Kilkenny City has more than 37 times the value of a vote in our Constituency.

To contest an election in a Borough of less than 5,000 electors costs the candidate not more than £470 in election expenses. An election in an average County Constituency costs about £1,200, but every election in the Romford Division costs each candidate well over £5,000.

The following diagram* shows at a glance the political history of the Division since 1885 :—

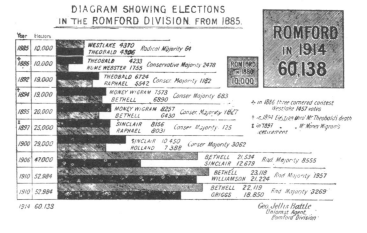

DIAGRAM SHOWING ELECTIONS IN THE ROMFORD DIVISION FROM 1885.

INDEPENDENT ORDER OF ODDFELLOWS.

MANCHESTER UNITY.

LOYAL " BRITANNIC " LODGE, No. 1685.

The Hornchurch Loyal Britannic Lodge of Oddfellows has a history dating back to the year 1846, and it possesses records of a Grand Jubilee celebration which was held on August 27, 1896. The following is an extract

* Mr. Battle, in addition to furnishing me with the details given in this chapter, has permitted the reproduction of his interesting diagram.

from a report of this event, taken from the PARISH MAGAZINE for October, 1896 :—

"The members of the Loyal Britannic Lodge of Oddfellows, M.U., celebrated their 50th anniversary on Thursday, August 27. The Order is one of the institutions of Hornchurch, as much so, perhaps, as the volunteer corps ; and just as on a big field-day everybody one meets in the village has stepped into uniform, so on Thursday everyone had assumed a blue or scarlet scarf or riband, or some elaborate insignia of the Order of Oddfellows. The village wore holiday aspect. Flaunting stretches of bunting everywhere over-shadowed the quaint architecture of the main street, and its white gables and overhanging storeys quite lost their charm for the visitor amid the crowd of mural devices. Soon after half-past one, a procession was formed at the Lodge house, the Bull Inn, and the Oddfellows paraded the village to the strains of the Artillery and Rifle band. The procession was headed by a carriage, in which rode Bros. G. Rayment and A. Bull, the two oldest officers, and Bros. L. Fry and Tarling, the two youngest members of the Lodge."

The celebrations included a cricket match and sports in Grey Towers Park, a dinner at the Drill Hall, at which the company numbered about 130, and a tea for the juvenile members.

The membership on the 31st December, 1916, was 370, and the funds amounted to £7,805.

The present officers of the Lodge are :—Trustees, Messrs. Thomas C. Howard, George Fry and John H. Pearce ; Treasurer, Mr. George Heath ; Secretary, Mr. Horace G. Fry, 9, Park Side Cottages, Hornchurch. The Lodge is held at the Bull Inn, High Street.

THE ROYAL JUBILEES AND THE CORONATIONS.

Queen Victoria's Jubilee of 1887, her Diamond Jubilee of 1897, the Coronation of King Edward VII. on August 9th, 1902, and of King George V. on June 22, 1911, were all loyally observed by the people of Hornchurch, and considerable sums of money were subscribed by the inhabitants for the celebrations. On each occasion the festivities included a dinner to the old folk and widows, to the school children tea and entertainments, and to all the parishioners a fête and sports in Grey Towers Park, concluding with a grand display of fireworks.

After paying all the expenses connected with these public festivities, the following sums of money were devoted to public and charitable purposes as permanent memorials :—

Jubilee 1887 :—The sum of £145 was subscribed to the Victoria Cottage Hospital, Romford, which was founded to commemorate the completion of 50 years of the reign of Queen Victoria.

Diamond Jubilee 1897 :—The sum of £52 was devoted to the founding of a Village Nursing Fund for Hornchurch.

Coronation of King Edward VII. :—£50 was given as a donation to the Victoria Cottage Hospital, Romford, and £10 to the Hornchurch Village Nursing Fund.

Coronation of King George V. :—£50 was placed on deposit at the London County and Westminster Bank at Romford, in the names of four Trustees, as the nucleus of a fund for the purchase of the Millfield, Hornchurch, as a Public Recreation Ground. If at the end of five years the purchase of the Millfield has not been decided upon, the fund to be devoted to such local charity or charities as the Trustees may decide. The Trustees appointed were : Messrs. Charles H. Baker, Thomas Gardner, James Robert Robertson, and W. Varco Williams.

THE COTTAGE HOMES OF THE PARISH OF ST. LEONARD, SHOREDITCH.

About a mile from the Church, on the Hornchurch Road, are situated the picturesque Homes provided by the Board of Guardians of Shoreditch for the accommodation of the children of that parish, who, through the misfortunes of their parents, become the necessary care of the State, in order that they may secure a good upbringing. These Homes constitute a self-contained village on a small scale, and that they formed the locale of Pett Ridge's novel " A Son of the State " adds not a little to their interest.

It would appear that as far back as the early 'forties feeling was rife that children under the care of local authorities should be separated from the environment

THE COTTAGE HOMES.

of Workhouses, and there is evidence that the Shoreditch Guardians were in the van of those who undertook measures to that desirable end. From an official report, dated 14 July 1892, I gather that from 1848 to 1854, a separate school existed at Enfield, which was afterwards transferred to new premises at Brentwood. In March 1877 Hackney and Shoreditch amalgamated to form the Brentwood School District, and one school was used for the children of both Unions, an arrangement which continued until March 1885. It then became necessary for the Shoreditch Guardians to establish a separate school. The children were temporarily housed at Harold Court, Harold Wood, until the completion of the present scheme at Hornchurch in 1889, the site, originally known as Harrow Lodge Estate, belonging to Mr. Edward Bousfield Dawson, and comprising 86 acres, with farm buildings, having been purchased by the Board in May 1886, at a cost of £6,300. Mr. F. J. Smith, F.R.I.B.A., was appointed Architect, and the building and equipment of the Homes was in charge of a Committee, of which Mr. R. G. Alabaster was chairman. He was also Chairman of the first Visiting Committee, and both Committees had the capable assistance of Mr. R. Clay as Clerk, a position which he still holds to-day. The undertaking was to include 11 cottages, probationary lodge, infirmary, schools, swimming bath, bakery, workshops, needleroom, stores, and administrative offices, together with accommodation for the Superintendent and Matron. Subsequently two additional cottages were provided for the isolation of sick children ; these are now used for small boys and infants.

In 1911 a Drill Hall and Gymnasium was erected.

The Local Government Board in January 1890 certified the Homes for the accommodation of 337 children ; the present accommodation provides for 425.

The original estimate for the cost of the building was £48,340. Sixty acres of ground are sublet to a local farmer, and there is a reservation of plots sufficient to raise all the garden produce necessary for the Homes. To persons unacquainted with the Cottage Homes, it may be difficult to comprehend the many achievements in the direction of increasing the value of these children as citizens. The first requirement is the presence of a Superintendent and a Matron, persons imbued with the greatest interest in the children and anxious to seize every opportunity for aiding them throughout their term at the Homes, and in after life. In these capacities, Mr. and Mrs. J. Cowley acted from the inception of the Homes until the close of 1911, when they retired, having won the esteem of the Board, the devotion of their colleagues and the confidence of the hundreds of youngsters who passed through their hands. The Homes then came under the direction of the present Superintendent and Matron, Mr. and Mrs. H. E. Steed, who are maintaining the traditions of their predecessors in every respect.

The idea behind the institution is that the life of the children shall be modelled, as nearly as possible, to the outside domestic ideal, and to this end foster parents for each of the cottage houses are appointed with care. There are 13 of these cottages, all detached, each constituting a " home " in itself, and having a distinctive name. In those set apart for big boys, the Board provides a foster-father and a foster-mother—man and wife. The girls are separately housed under the care of a foster-mother in each cottage. who is assisted by the elder girls, and who thus inculcates at first-hand the correct principles of house management. The smaller boys and infants are also under the control and guidance of foster-mothers, and to meet the necessities of the case paid helpers are provided to assist with the handling of the tiny tots.

During the hours usually devoted to the school life of a child, inmates of the Homes are taught in the school which forms a central feature of the establishment.

At other times specialised occupation and instruction is arranged—for the boys, who are taught bakery, gardening, shoemaking, painting, tailoring, and carpentry, and for the girls, who are instructed in cookery, laundry work, needlework and general domestic economy. By these means a dual purpose is served —the children contribute their quota to the self-maintenance of the Homes, at the same time being fitted for some definite employment in after life, in accordance with their more pronounced tastes or aptitudes.

By no means the least feature of this scheme of instruction is the work of the boys' band, under the direction of Mr. H. W. Alden. Some 40 boy performers are regularly in training. Apart from their usefulness in providing musical entertainment within the Homes, the lads are being fitted to take their places in military bands, in which direction many former inmates have already found their livelihoods.

The Drill Hall is a valuable asset to the scheme. Organised instruction in physical training is given to all who are physically fit by Mr. G. Smith.

The school is inspected by the Board of Education, under arrangement with the Local Government Board.

The well-equipped Infirmary, in charge of Miss K, Willis, not only deals with an average of 20 in-patients. but daily treats about 80 out-patients for minor ills.

It is indeed hard to realise the fulness of effort put forward on behalf of these youngsters. The annual Sports Day reveals to some extent the untiring devotion of all concerned with their upbringing, particularly the self-imposed tasks of the head teachers, Miss Pyatt. and Mr. H. H. W. Brice, who do not allow the nature of the institution in any way to stultify that aim which they have in common with all educational workers of to-day.

Nor is the spiritual welfare of the children neglected. A portion of the school premises is consecrated to Divine Worship, the Rev. Herbert Dale (vicar of Hornchurch) officiating as Chaplain. Regular services are held here, and an annual confirmation, with an average of 60 candidates, takes place in the Chapel of the Homes.

It is safe to say that nothing needful for the proper training and general welfare of the children is overlooked. With an eye to useful occupation, of a type likely to interest the children, the daily routine of the Cottage Homes works easily with scarcely any suggestion to remind the little ones that they live under different circumstances to those of their more fortunate fellows. In this connection the avoidance of any set uniform clothing is noticeable, a point on which the governing body is to be congratulated.

Sent out on to the broader walks of life, after scrupulous investigation of places of possible employment, each child is provided with necessary clothing, etc., for a year, and its future is followed with interest. And so they start on their careers, scattered, in some cases, to the furthermost bounds of our dominions, but united in a common recollection of early days at Hornchurch, and not the least satisfactory feature to the Board and Officers is the receipt of frequent letters from ' old boys ' and ' old girls,' and the return visits which are made as opportunity serves. At the present time, when the Call of Empire has brought countless men from far off climes to bear their share in the struggle for our imperial safety, many ' old boys ' are passing through the Metropolis as soldiers in colonial contingents, and not a few have already paid the price of personal sacrifice.

If we should pay a visit to the Homes let us forget that it is a rate-supported institution, and that the little ones are the children of adversity. Let us ask ourselves how well the children compare with those whom we term their " more fortunate " fellows. Short of a real mother's particular love and care, which, after all, no legislation can ever really replace, what do these little ones lack ? What more could the community do for them. The answer is—Nothing !

The present Committee for the Cottage Homes is as follows :—Mr. P. Kelleher, Chairman ; Mr. G. W. Bailey, Vice-Chairman ; Mrs. H. Girling, Mr. W. Bradley, Mr. J. L. Cooke, Mr. E. Cooper, Mr. C. J. English, Mr. S. Knightly, Mr. G. Tyrie, Mr. E. J. Wakeling, Mr. C. Wilton, and Mr. G. F. Wood.

THE NATIONAL BRITISH WOMEN'S TEMPERANCE ASSOCIATION.

A branch of this association was formed in Hornchurch in 1905, and, during the twelve years which have since intervened, has carried on an active and vigorous temperance campaign, more particularly among the women of the parish. In addition to the public meetings which have been held from time to time, there have been many garden and drawing room meetings, and these have greatly helped to further the principles of total abstinence advocated by the association.

During the first two years of the war, the members established a rest room in North Street, where they carried on an excellent work in supplying light refreshment, and providing games and literature for the troops quartered in the village. While the First Sportsman's Battalion was in training at Grey Towers, the rest room was nightly filled with soldiers, who greatly appreciated the arrangements made for their comfort. On their departure, the Pioneers Battalion was similarly catered for, as was also the New Zealand contingent in the early days of their occupation of Grey Towers Camp.

The Officers and Committee of the association for 1916–1917 were :—President, Miss Keighley ; Vice-Presidents, Mrs. Perfect and Mrs. Dowse ; Hon. Secretary, Miss Fardell ; Hon. Treasurer and Literature Secretary, Mrs. Hadler ; Committee, Mrs. Beharell, Mrs. Bridges, Mrs. Dohoo, Mrs. Haywood, Mrs. Hinton, Mrs. Major, Mrs. Sutton.

EDWARD THE CONFESSOR LODGE OF FREEMASONS.

The Edward the Confessor Lodge of Freemasons, which was founded in 1916, combines at one and the same time the earliest and latest historical association with our old village, for not only is this most recently consecrated Essex Lodge named after the Confessor, but its members claim him as a brother Freemason.

The ancient history of Freemasonry in Hornchurch is, moreover, not exhausted by this linking up of the Craft with the great Saxon King and Saint, for it can be shown that a previous Masonic Lodge existed in Hornchurch as far back as the year 1734. It is thus referred to in masonic records :—

"The Lodge was consecrated in 1734 and met at the Red Lion, Hornchurch, its number being 182. When Grand Lodge held its great revision in 1740 this number was altered to 169, and this was again changed in 1755 to 103. Under this number, for reasons unknown and unrecorded at Grand Lodge, it was erased in the year 1769, having thus existed for a space of 35 years."

The foundation of the Edward the Confessor Lodge arose out of an informal meeting of four Hornchurch Freemasons in 1916, and as the outcome of their deliberations a meeting of Freemasons resident in the locality was held on March 27, 1916, at Suffolk House, in the High Street, at which it was decided that a Lodge should be founded in Hornchurch. The usual formalities then followed, and in due course a warrant was applied for and obtained.

In December, 1916, the Edward the Confessor Lodge was consecrated by Bro. the Right Hon. Mark Lockwood, P.C., C.V.O., M.P. (now Lord Lambourne), Provincial Grand Master of Essex. This ceremony took place at the Great Eastern Hotel, Bishopsgate, London, E.C., The Provincial Grand Master was assisted by Bros. W. Rains Webster, Prov.S.G.W. ; Owen H. Clarke, Prov.J.G.W. ; Rev. J. Bishop Marsh, Prov.G.C. ; Thos. J. Ralling, P.G.D., Prov.G.Sec. ; Victor Taylor, Prov.G.D.C. ; R. Haward Ives, P.P.G.W.; and A. W. Martin, Prov.G.Tyler.

In the course of an oration delivered by the Prov. G. Chaplain, the following interesting reference was made to the connection of the name of Edward the Confessor with the new Lodge :—

"Let us not, then, forget that this Lodge is consecrated in each and every one of its parts to show that Freemasonry is not only illustrated by symbols but veiled in allegory. This Lodge also bears the honoured name of King Edward the Confessor, a man of simple faith and devotional practice. Hornchurch is rightly proud that it can be said of him that he was born there.   Green, the historian, writes : ' A halo of tenderness, spread in after time round this last king of the old English stock, legends told of his pious simplicity, his gentleness of mood and holiness that gained him the name of Confessor.'   He devoted personal attention to the foundations of the great monastery and church of St. Peter at Westminster ;   he saw its consecration on Holy Innocents' Day in the year 1065, and in the following month left this earthly abode for the heavenly temple above. Parts of the original Norman work of Edward the Confessor may still be seen in the crypt of the Chapter House of Westminster Abbey, and in the arches that prolong the eastern walk of the Cloister.   Will such a life as his, and such a work as the building up of a great Temple fail to be an incentive to the W.M., the Officers and Brethren of this Lodge of Edward the Confessor."

Freemasonry also associates the legend of the giving of the ring to the beggar man by Edward the Confessor with their Craft, and claims that the incident occurred as the King was returning from a ceremonial in the neighbourhood, and that having disposed of all the money on his person at that ceremony for charitable purposes, as was the custom with Freemasons in those days, he was met by the beggar man (who, it is claimed, was also a Mason), and having no alms to bestow upon him, he took the ring from his finger and gave it to the beggar, with the words " Have a ring."*

The ceremony of installation was performed by the Prov. Grand Secretary, Bro. T. J. Ralling, P.G.D., who installed Bro. Charles J. Beharell as the first W.M.

The Worshipful Master then appointed and invested his officers as follows :—Bros. Alfred Robertson, S.W. ; John Braid, J.W. ; J. W. Ewing, Treasurer ; Rev. A. J. Parry, P.P.G.C., Secretary ; E. Featherstone Griffin, as acting I.P.M. ; E. F. Williams, D.C. ; James Bauckham, S.D. ; W. J. Eales, J.D. ; Charles Living, I.G. ; John Downton, junr., Steward.

There was a very large muster of visitors, including, among the Installed Masters, Bros. the Bishop of Barking, P.G.C. ; Rev. F. S. Paynter, A.G.C. ; Leo Taylor, P.A.G.D.C. ; W. Harvey, A.G.P. ; Dr. T. Scoresby-Jackson, P.P.G.D. ; A. Holmes, P.P.G.D. ; H. W. Stride, P.P.G.Supt. Works ; Lieut. Percy J. Weston, P.P.A.G.D.C. ; F. W. Ivey, L.R. ; J. J Bassett, L.R. ; A. Carter, L.R. ; H. Cope, L.R. ; W. P

* The generally accepted version of this legendary story will be found on page 57.

Wilson, E. Pitt, George Gall, James P. Barnett, A. A. Wallett, T. Horwood, C. J. Manché, R. C. Flint, S. A. Hatcher, G. S. Evans, and F. Pulverman.

At the conclusion of the Lodge proceedings there was a dinner in the Hamilton Hall, under the presidency of the W.M. The toast of " The Provincial Grand Master " was accorded musical honours, the New Zealand members of the Forces present, and there were many, rendering it in the Maori language.

This was probably the first occasion on which the Maori language was ever used at a Masonic consecration in England. The New Zealand Contingent stationed in England have a very close relationship with the Edward the Confessor Lodge, and it is of interest to record that the first initiate of the Lodge was one of their officers, viz. :—Bro. Gordon H. Forsythe, Captain and Adjutant of the New Zealand Convalescent Hospital.

The Lodge meets at the Council Hall, Billet Lane, Hornchurch.

VILLAGE CRICKET.

Hornchurch has always been well to the fore in the realms of sport, but it is in the national game of cricket that " Our Village " has especially excelled.

There are perhaps few villages that can boast of a record dating back to the eighteenth century, but I am able to claim that distinction for Hornchurch. In " Say's Weekly Journal " for September 4th, 1784, appears the following report :—

"Last Monday se'nnight* a Match of Cricket was played at Knavestock in Essex by the United Clubs of Kennington & Bow against the Hornchurch Club, which was won with great ease by the latter, and last Monday a second Match of Cricket was played at Bow in Middlesex by the same parties, when victory, with the same ease & condescension as before, yielded the palm to the Hornchurch Club, which (considering that this is the second season of its practising) displayed such a superior degree of skill in the various parts of the game, that not only afforded great pleasure to, but really astonished, the spectators."

Early in the last century, Hornchurch was one of the great cricketing centres of the county. There would

* Fortnight.

appear to be little doubt that the celebrated pitch in Grey Towers Park was well over 100 years old when it was last played upon in 1914. Prior to 1876, when Colonel Holmes built and occupied "Grey Towers," the cricket field formed part of the estate of "Langtons," which, at the time the Bearblock Eleven made it famous, was owned by Mrs. Massu. In those days a cricket match in Hornchurch was an event of such importance that the forge hammers at "Fairkytes" Foundry ceased to beat, and all the village kept high holiday. I have it on the testimony of many of the old inhabitants that on match days a string of carriages, brakes, and drags reached all up and down the High Street, from the Cricketers' Inn to the White Hart Hotel, and that the spectators often numbered several thousands. The cricket elevens were entertained alternatively at the "Bull Inn" and the "White Hart." Booths and marquees were erected in the Park, where food and refreshment was dispensed to the eager and interesting throng of cricket enthusiasts, many of whom came very long distances to witness the game. It is quite possible, too, that some of them had more than a passing interest in the sport of the day, for it was not always that cricket was played only for the honour of the game, as it is to-day. Many matches were played for valuable money stakes, and wagering on the result was as common in those days as is betting on horse racing at the present time.

Wagering on Cricket Matches.

In the 18th century cricket became so much the subject of wagering, that in 1748 it was sought to put it down by Act of Parliament, but the Court of King's Bench decided in its favour. Wagering continued to increase until the first quarter of the 19th century, when matches were often played for stakes of 500 to 1,000 guineas a side.

A match in which betting is recorded is given in the following curious report of a match which took place at Hornchurch in the year 1825 :—

"On Tuesday last the return Match of Cricket was played at Hornchurch Essex, between Eleven Gentlemen of the above

Parish, and Eleven Gentlemen of Fobbing and adjacent parishes, which terminated in the following manner :—

Hornchurch	1st	Innings	85	Fobbing	42
Do.	2nd	do.	87	do.	70
			172		112
	Majority		60		

"In consequence of the day closing, the Fobbing gentlemen could not have their last innings completed by 5 wickets to go down, but the majority being 60 runs in favour of Hornchurch, the Fobbing gave up the Match as lost ; *therefore all bets may be decided by the above statement.* The gentlemen then retired to the Bull Inn, where, after partaking of a most excellent dinner, provided by Mr. Gooch, the Landlord, they were amused by some excellent songs, and the evening passed off with the greatest conviviality, for which all parties were much indebted to the Fobbing gentlemen. Their handsome conduct throughout both Matches cannot be too highly spoken of."

Hornchurch v. All Essex.

It was between the years 1822 and 1834 that the Hornchurch Club so greatly distinguished itself. In 1829 it was recorded that "the Hornchurch players had not been beaten for seven years," and so great was their prowess in the field that in that year they challenged "all Essex." The challenge was not taken up, but in the following year—1830—they again issued their challenge to the county, which on that occasion was accepted. The challenge and its acceptance appeared in the press in the following terms :—

The Challenge :—" The gentlemen of the Hornchurch Club who, with one exception, all live in that Parish, have repeated their readiness to meet any eleven players actually residing in this county, with the proviso that the matches be played at Hornchurch, and within 30 miles of that place."

The Acceptance ;—" The challenge, which the Hornchurch cricketers gave to the county of Essex some time since, has been met by the well-known Tom Rounding, on behalf of the county —who has engaged to provide eleven gentlemen to play Hornchurch on Thursday next, 1st July, at Woodford Wells, when good sport is contemplated by the lovers of the manly pastime."

The match resulted in an easy win on the first innings for our village, Hornchurch scoring 89, and Essex 19 in the first innings and 41 in the second innings for the loss of five wickets.

In 1829–1830, there are records of matches between

Hornchurch and most of the first class London clubs, including the Albion Islington and the Chelsea Wellington. They also encountered the East Surrey Club and the West Essex Club (for many years the best known eleven in the county), and in most of these encounters Hornchurch proved victorious.

Hornchurch v. M.C.C.

It was in 1831 that our village club reached the high water mark of their ambition by challenging the Marylebone Cricket Club. When it is borne in mind that the M.C.C. was the foremost Cricket Club in England, that it published the first code of laws for the game, and that it was then, as now, the ruling and arbitrary authority in cricket affairs, we can form some idea of the place Hornchurch held in the cricket world, when such a Club considered them worthy opponents, and accepted their challenge for two matches. In the first match, played at Lord's Cricket Ground in London, on June 10th, 1831, Hornchurch put up a very creditable show, the result being a draw, which could not be said to be by any means in favour of the M.C.C., the scores being :—M.C.C. 71 and 58, and Hornchurch 61 and 7 for no wicket. This match was referred to in the press as follows :—" That spirited little Club of Hornchurch, having been successful for several seasons in conquering all they have had to compete with, amongst which were the Islington Albion, East Surrey, Chelsea, Dartford, and others of minor importance, have now had the courage to challenge the Marylebone Club, which match commenced on Thursday last, the 10th inst., in the presence of a large assemblage of amateurs, amongst whom were the celebrated Pilchs, Caldecourt, etc., who were surprised to witness the stumps of the *crack club* lowered for so few runs by a country parish club, particularly those of Cobbett and Bayley. Mr. John Stevens' play was the admiration of the whole company, as he is one of the old school, and between 60 and 70 years of age."

In the second match, played at Langtons on August 25th, 1831, before a company of about 3,000 people,

Hornchurch were badly beaten, the scores being :—
M.C.C. 78 and 118, and Hornchurch 54 and 39.

Their defeat by the M.C.C. in no way disheartened our famous village players, for in 1832 we find them playing in great style at Langtons Park against Ingatestone. This match was thus reported :—

"The Hornchurch gentlemen were put in first, their opponents winning the toss, &, at half past three o'clock, only four of their wickets were down, & the score standing at 237, the Ingatestone gentlemen thought proper to relinquish the match."

Hornchurch v. West Essex.

In the same year Hornchurch defeated Chelmsford, and in 1834 at Navestock they obtained an easy victory over West Essex* in the first innings, the scores being West Essex 39, Hornchurch 118. In that match two of the Bearblocks (W. and J.) played for West Essex, while P. Bearblock played for the village. The county eleven did well in the second innings, which is recorded as follows :—

"West Essex had scored 116 in the second innings at 7 o'clock, when we left the ground. Four of their men were out, but Mr. J. Bearblock still retained his bat, from which he had scored 72 *notches*."

The records at my disposal at this period of the club's existence do not go beyond 1834, but it is evident that for several years our village players were the undoubted champions of the county. It is hardly conceivable that a Club which had achieved such remarkable success would be likely to cease their activities, and in all probability they retained their proud position in the county for many years afterwards.

I have no other reliable records until 1876. In the 'seventies Hornchurch amalgamated with Upminster, under the style of the Hornchurch and Upminster United Cricket Club. This went on for some time, and later on Hornchurch again had its own village club, but up to the year 1884 nothing exceptional occurred, though occasionally some good cricket was recorded.

* In the *Victoria History of Essex* appears the following note with reference to this West Essex Club :—"The ground at Navestock Green throughout the greater part of the 19th century was the scene of 'West Essex' cricket, for many years the best known Club in the county "

After the year 1884 there was no village club in Hornchurch for nearly five years, but in November, 1889, a new Club was formed, of which the first officers were :—President, Major Holmes ; Vice-Presidents, Rev. Robert Johnson, Mr. Thomas Gardner, and Mr. E. T. Helme ; Captain, Mr. J. R. Robertson ; Vice-Captain, Mr. E. G. Bratchell ; Hon. Secretary, Mr. Walter Dendy ; and Hon. Treasurer, Mr. F. Jenvey.

The Club commenced its first season on June 20th, 1890, in a match against St. George's Hospital, in which Hornchurch won easily, the scores being :—St. George's 58, Hornchurch 88 for six wickets.

Coming of Age Dinner.

The coming of age of this new club was celebrated on May 7th, 1910, by a great dinner at the Drill Hall, Hornchurch, which was attended by a large number of past and present members, among them being :—Mr. Charles Godfrey, Captain of the old Club for several seasons ; Mr. Albert Holmes, Mr. S. de Winton, of the Gloucester XI., Mr. F. Jenvey, Mr. H. W. Stride and Mr Arthur Forrester, Hon. Sec. of the Club in 1891-2-3-5-6 ; Mr. O. R. Borradaile, Secretary of the Essex County Cricket Club, was also present.

Mr. Thos. Gardner occupied the chair, and was supported by Mr. J. R. Robertson, Mr. Edgar G. Bratchell, and Mr. J. Poupart as Vice-Chairmen.

In the course of the speeches delivered during the evening many interesting details concerning the club were disclosed, some of which are as follows :—

It was announced that Mr. J. R. Robertson had been Captain of the Club since its inception in 1889 ; that Colonel Henry Holmes had filled the office of President, and Mr. Thomas Gardner that of Vice-President for the whole of the 21 years.

Mr. W. Varco W.lliams had been a Vice-President since 1902. Only four Hon. Secretaries had been elected during the existence of the Club, viz.:—Mr. Walter Dendy, Mr. Arthur L. Forrester, Mr. Stanhope Haynes, and the present Hon. Sec., Mr. E. G. Bratchell, who had filled that office for the past 13 years.

On nine occasions the Club had been matched against the Essex Club & Ground, two of those matches having been played at Hornchurch. Although the village had not succeeded in winning any of these contests, they had in three of them compiled the creditable scores of 147, 164 & 170, and on one occasion lost by only 8 runs. The scores in that match, which took place in 1910, were Essex 131, Hornchurch 123.

During the 21 years 381 matches had been played, and of these 183 had been won, 138 lost, and 60 drawn.

Three centuries had been scored for the Club, viz :—by Mr. Bert G. Bratchell—100 against East Ham Atlas ; Mr. H. W. Stride, 106 not out, against Leyton ; and Mr. H. J. Harris, 105, not out, against Dagenham.

The highest batting average was made by Mr. H. J. Harper in 1902, his record being 32.2.

The largest number of runs scored by any individual member in any one season was 361 by Mr. A. L. Forrester.

Mr. J. R. Robertson, in the twentieth year of his Captaincy, headed the batting averages ; his highest individual score being 65.

The Club had possessed many good bowlers in the course of its long life, not the least of them being Mr. G. Adams, who had headed the bowling averages four times within the previous five years. But the record of Mr. Edgar G. Bratchell with the leather was the most remarkable in the annals of the Club. He had bowled 3,940 overs, and had captured 1,115 wickets for 8,328 runs, his average being 7.46. In addition to this he had the distinction of having scored more runs than any other member, his total being 2,726.

In 1911 the brothers Bratchell both beat Mr. A. L. Forrester's record aggregate, viz. :—E. G. Bratchell, 400, and B. G. Bratchell 418 ; and in that same year E. G. B. made 103 not out—against Harold Wood.

It will be seen that our cricketers of this day have worthily upheld the traditions of their forebears ; but the glories of the 'thirties of last century can never return, for what Hornchurch then did " off its own bat " can now only be attempted through the medium of County Cricket.

On the death of Colonel Holmes in 1913 Mr. Thomas Gardner was elected President of the Club.

The activities of the Club were continued until the season of 1914, when the Great War made it impossible for the members to indulge in the national game. The mimic fights of the cricket field have now given place to the sterner fight of " Right versus Might " on the field of battle ; and in that grim struggle no less than twelve members of the Village Club have been engaged, viz. :—

George Adams, Newton Adams, C. H. Baker, jun.,* R. Dawson, G. W. Franklin, jun.,* A. V. Gentry, C. Lovett, A. A. Mather, J. Moss, E. H. Robinson, A. F. G. Ruston and R. F. Stroud.

THE ROYAL LIBERTY OF HAVERING.

This ancient Liberty was ruled by a High Steward, Deputy Steward, Clerk of the Peace, and a Coroner, and had the singular privilege of appointing one of its own magistrates by popular suffrage.† It was bounded by the Becontree, Ongar, and Chafford Hundreds, and extended to the Thames on the south, where it narrowed to less than a mile in width. It was about $4\frac{1}{2}$ miles from east to west, and about 9 miles from north to south.

The whole of this district was, in the earliest ages, one Manor under the King, and formed part of the Becontree Hundred, but as the Palace at Havering gradually grew into greater importance, and became more frequently a place of royal resort, it was erected into a Liberty, with courts of its own to administer justice in ecclesiastical, civil and criminal matters, even to inflicting the punishment of death.‡

The Liberty was divided into seven wards, and contained seventeen Manors, which are given in Morant's *History of Essex* as under :—

Wards —1 Havering, 2 North End, 3 Noke Hill, 3 Collier Row, 5 Harold's Wood, 6 Romford Town, 7 South End.

The Manors :—

On the North :—1 Havering-atte-Bower.
              2 Pirgo.
              3 Dagenhams (Dagnams)

* The names of two of these brave lads have been added to the Nation's Roll of Honour, viz. :—C. H. Baker and G. W. Franklin, who have fallen in action. —C. F. P.

† The High Steward and Deputy Steward were appointed by the Crown and later by the Lord of the Manor. The third J.P. was elected by the inhabitants.

‡ Coller's *People's History of Essex* (1861)

4 Cockerells.
5 Gosayes (Gooses).
6 Uphavering or Gobions.
7 Reedon or Ridden Court.
8 Manor of Romford or Mannys (Mawney's).
9 Geddyng Hall (Gidea Hall), East House, and Bedfords.
10 Stewards
11 Marks.

*On the South :—12 Nelmes.
13 Lees Gardens.
14 Maylerds.
15 Brettons.
16 Suttons.
17 Dovers.

The formation of the Liberty and the grant of the famous Charter was made in 1465, in the reign of Edward IV., although some privileges appear to have been previously enjoyed.

Hornchurch men in the past were certainly favoured individuals, by reason of their living within the limits of the Royal Liberty, of which the actual town† of Hornchurch was the capital. Not only were the privileges within the said Liberty of a real and tangible sort, but they had certain other privileges which extended beyond the confines of the Liberty. The Seal of the Havering Liberty represents a Castle with a ring placed under it, with this inscription :—" Sigillum Manerii de Havering-atte-Bower." Tenants and inhabitants of this Liberty, by having these arms painted on their wagons and carts, had the privilege of exemption from paying the toll of the City of London, could pass toll free through all gates, roads, or bridges where dues were claimed, and were admitted free at all markets and fairs in the kingdom.

I am able to reproduce here, by courtesy of Major A. B. Bamford, who has in his possession the original

* It will be noticed that *Morant* does not include Hornchurch Hall in his list as a separate Manor, see page 32.
† Hornchurch is frequently referred to in old records as a town, see instances on pages 17 and 25.

document, a copy of the DOCQUET which was issued to an inhabitant of the Liberty :—

DOCQUET.

Manor of Havering-atte-Bower, in Essex.

Whereas the said Manor of Havering-atte-Bower is and from time out of mind hath been part of the Ancient Demesne Lands of the Crown of that part of Great Britain called England, and therefore by the Laws and customs of this Realm all Tenants of the said Manor and also all inhabitants residing and dwelling therein amongst divers other Privileges have by all the times aforesaid been and are and by the Said Laws and Customs are to be toll free and quit and discharged from payment of any Toll Pontage Murage or Passage in any City Borough, Town Fair, Market, or other place whatsoever. These are to give you knowledge that John Shuttleworth, the bearer hereof, is one of the Tenants of the Said Manor and therefore he is to be free from payment of any Toll, Pontage, Murage or Passage as aforesaid. In witness whereof the Common Seal of the Manor aforesaid is hereunto set and affixed the first day of January, in the Twentieth Year of the Reign of our Sovereign Lord George the Second, by the Grace of God of the United Kingdom of Great Braitain and Ireland King Defender of the Faith And in the year of our Lord One Thousand Seven Hundred and Forty-six.

Champion Branfill,
Deputy Steward.

In 1828 the Royal Manor of Havering was purchased by Hugh McIntosh, Esq., who was succeeded by the late David McIntosh, Esq., whose widow, Mrs. McIntosh, is now Lady of the Manor. Mr. Terry thus describes the remarkable sale of the ancient Liberty :—

" This Royal Manor was, on the 23rd September, 1828, put up in two lots to be sold by public auction, with all its peculiar rights and prerogatives, including the power of appointing judges and administrators of the laws of the Liberty, and the whole was purchased of the Crown by Hugh McIntosh, Esq. . . . The Lordship includes not only the ownership of about 1,530 acres, but also the peculiar manorial jurisdiction of upwards of 16,000 Acres. Tnis Royal Manor was put up for auction to go to the highest bidder. It was not the land only that was sold, but the prerogatives of the Crown were sold too. Seldom has it fallen to the lot of the auctioneer's hammer to knock down to a bidder at a sale the power of appointing judges and administering laws. So that what is by theory of our constitution a Royal duty and responsibility, was disposed of to anyone irrespective of anything else, than that he was able and willing to bid the highest sum at the auction."

THE DIOCESE OF CHELMSFORD.

Essex has seen more changes in regard to its Diocese than any other county in England. For many centuries it formed part of the Diocese of London, but in 1836 Essex and Hertfordshire were detached from London and added to the Diocese of Rochester. Both counties were in 1877 separated from Rochester, and together formed the newly created Diocese of St. Albans, and from that year to 1913 three Bishops reigned over the Diocese, viz. :—Bishop Claughton, Bishop Festing, and Bishop Jacob.

In 1913 Essex was separated from the Diocese of St. Albans and became the Diocese of Chelmsford.

Dr. J. E. Watts-Ditchfield, the first and present Bishop of Chelmsford, was consecrated in St. Paul's Cathedral on St. Matthias' Day, February 24th, 1914, and was enthroned in the Cathedral Church of Chelmsford on St. George's Day, April 23rd, 1914.

The Old Archway, High Street.

Hornchurch Hall

CHURCH AND DELL HORNCHURCH

LIST OF ILLUSTRATIONS.

INDEX.